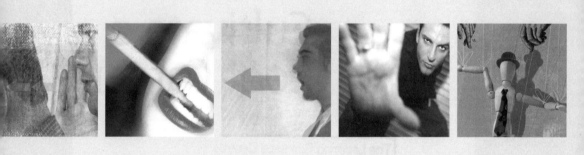

52 brilliantideas

one good idea can change your life...

Cultivate a Cool Career

Ken Langdon

Contents

Brilliant features

Each chapter of this book is designed to provide you with an inspirational idea that you can read quickly and put into practice straight away.

Throughout you'll find four features that will help you to get right to the heart of the idea:

- *Try another idea* If this idea looks like a life-changer then there's no time to lose. *Try another idea* will point you straight to a related tip to expand and enhance the first.

- *Here's an idea for you* Give it a go – right here, right now – and get an idea of how well you're doing so far.

- *Defining ideas* Words of wisdom from masters and mistresses of the art, plus some interesting hangers-on.

- *How did it go?* If at first you do succeed try to hide your amazement. If, on the other hand, you don't this is where you'll find a Q and A that highlights common problems and how to get over them.

Introduction

Your career needs the sort of care and attention that a passionate gardener gives to her plants. As high fliers perform their day-to-day activities, they also keep a weather eye on their careers. They cultivate good relationships with powerful people who can help them and they cultivate the skills and techniques that improve performance. That way they bring their careers to glorious fruition at the top of their chosen organisation.

So what distinguishes those who make it to the top, and those who languish in a job that doesn't stretch them, or give them the rewards they crave? Yes OK, it's skills and knowledge but it's also flair and you can develop flair.

Flair increases with the number of times you exercise it: so take risks and think outside the square. Throughout my conversations with top people I have found this to be a theme. Remember this mantra:

> *'It is easier to ask for forgiveness than it is to ask for permission.'*

Ambitious people do not wait for a sluggish management to come round to their way of thinking. They make things happen, and then if the risk goes wrong they own up and ask for forgiveness. The risk-averse and craven manager asks for permission to act. If this is denied he is stuffed. Either he goes ahead anyway against specific instructions, or, more likely, he leaves well alone and misses out on a chance to shine.

Just think for a moment about how much of your career is left to chance. It depends on who happens to be your boss when you get promoted, for example, and who likes or dislikes him or her. It depends on the exigencies of the products and services you deliver and the markets you deliver them into. It depends on the economic climate and even who is in political control of the country. All of these are, to say the least, chancy. You have some control over some of these elements, but certainly not over them all.

So what do you do when you're seeking to achieve a difficult business objective with a fair degree of uncertainty? Why, you make a plan of course. You look at other people's experience and develop a career strategy.

This book is about such a strategy and how top people have found the key to different aspects of building careers. It does not pretend that the world is just, or that it owes you a living. Rather it takes on the world as it is. It looks at how you get as much control as you can over a world where life is mostly froth and bubble.

I do not ignore the fact that success is built on success. If you want a promotion you have to perform to specification in your current role. Some of the ideas, therefore, are to do with improving performance; but they are all illustrations of how others have nurtured a humble acorn into a mighty oak standing head and shoulders above the rest of the forest.

1

Face it, you are you and they are them

Take a positive, practical but sceptical attitude to your organisation. Don't expect to spend your whole career in one organisation and don't trip over internal politics.

Are you in the right place? People are happier and work better when they can identify with the objectives of the organisation they work for.

It is hard to get up in the morning with energy and enthusiasm if you feel that your work contributes to something you couldn't care less about. Make sure you are working for an organisation that is doing something worthwhile and is likely to be successful. You are much more likely to build a career there.

If right now you're working towards a goal that neither interests you nor inspires you, you've got to make a change. It's up to you. Your career is a key element in your way of life and your general happiness; if you are in the wrong place get out of it.

Here's an idea for you... It is best for your boss to think that other people believe your good ideas are his. You, on the other hand, should ensure people know that your ideas and your boss's good ideas are both yours.

YOU HAVE OUR UNDIVIDED LOYALTY

until it doesn't suit us

Now let's look at the other side of the coin – the organisation itself. Your organisation is probably chaotic, either all the time, or sometimes, or in places. This is both a problem and an opportunity for the career minded. This chaos means that whatever it says about looking after you and your career, your company may very well not be able to live up to its promises. Organisations, for example, have to take technological change on board if they are to survive even if it costs careers. In short, the organisation has to look after itself in a businesslike way, so you need to look after yourself in a similarly objective and professional way.

And circumstances change. A promise made to a member of staff in good faith may suddenly become impractical. In this environment the safest view to take of your organisation is that you owe it your loyal support only for as long as your objectives and the organisation's can co-exist. Career planning is now a question of a number of jobs rather than a simple progression up a single organisation. Companies don't offer jobs for life and most successful careerists will change employers from time to time. Keep an open mind and don't get so set in your ways that you get caught out by a reorganisation in which you find yourself 'Co-ordinator of Long-term Planning'. Such a post almost certainly means that you are no longer part of those long-term plans. I'm certainly not encouraging you to be dishonest yourself. But be warned that others are sometimes going to use 'their best intentions' to meet their obligations.

Defining idea... *'Success has many fathers, failure is an orphan.'*

Career players take integrity very seriously. They do not, however, ignore the facts of the new world – the company man is extinct. The key phrase now is 'fluidity of labour'.

If you do want to change, have a look at IDEA 14, *Send an inside salesperson*. It's about selling yourself.

Try another idea...

NURTURE THE POLITICIAN WITHIN YOU

It is not possible for any organisation to exist without some form of internal politics. People often have conflicting agendas and objectives. Face it. Don't make a decision on behalf of an organisation without paying attention to what the implications are for you. If company politics permeate every decision that affects your career, you should face another brutal fact: *in company politics the competition is your colleagues.* After all, this is more than a matter of survival. The Vicar of Bray played his organisation's politics well and survived, but he never made it to bishop. My Dad, watching the politics that my mother got into in a small local church, was heard to murmur, 'The more I see of Christians, the more sorry I feel for the lions.' If the Church cannot avoid internal politics and strife, what chance has a capitalist corporation?

FINALLY

So, it's a question of 'us and them', or rather, remembering what we have said about your colleagues, of 'me and them'. Take responsibility for your own career, and work on the basis that no one else will.

'Except in poker, bridge and similar play period activities: don't con anybody. Not your spouse, not your children, not your employees, not your customers, not your stockholders, not your boss, not your associates, not your suppliers, not your regulatory authorities, not even your competitors.'
ROBERT TOWNSEND, Avis CEO

Defining idea...

How did it go?

Q **I have started to look at my colleagues as the enemy in career terms. It is tending to make me avoid contact with them in less guarded situations like over lunch or drink after work? Is this right?**

A *No. Such gatherings are an important source of information – and you need to know your enemy. These occasions also often present opportunities to do a bit of internal politicking. Just make sure you obey the salesperson's mantra – you must tell the truth and nothing but the truth, but show me someone who tells the whole truth and I'll show you a loser.*

Q **My new boss says that there are no politics in our part of the organisation and he doesn't want any to start.**

A *He's lying.*

Q **I hate company politics; it is energy sapping and wastes time. Do I have to think about them at all?**

A *I think you do. Have a look at the successful people around you. You will find they all talk about and think about their and other people's positions and abilities.*

2

Don't bury them in advice

To have a successful career, good managers need to build a reputation for breeding good people. They lead confident teams, limit the amount of advice they give and help their people solve their own problems.

Who would you rather work for, a person who keeps staff forever, or one who constantly loses people to better, more interesting positions? Exactly. If you are known to encourage your people to grow and have a reputation as a source of good people, the best people will beat a path to your door.

People come to their bosses in order to find the solution to a problem or some suggestions as to how they should set about exploiting an opportunity – right? Well not entirely, no. Sometimes they come to explore an idea while they make their own minds up. Sometimes they have a solution to the problem themselves and they want to validate it. In these situations hitting them with an avalanche of advice does more harm than good.

Here's an idea for you... **When someone comes to you for help with a problem, try to create a 'thinking partnership' for them rather than an advice clinic. Limit yourself to asking only questions; make no proposals during the session, no matter how long it takes. Look for incisive questions like 'If you could get over that hurdle, what would you do next?' Keep listening as they work out the actions they are going to take.**

(I was taught a number of exercises in this area on a course given by Penny Ferguson and with her permission have passed the 'thinking partnership' one on.)

After all, how do you know you have found the best solution? And what in the end are you trying to develop – your people's skills or a bunch of folk that do what you tell them? OK, eventually they'll believe that they can do your job better than you can, but that's better than having a bunch of grumblers who feel stuck in a dead-end job.

DON'T RUSH TO GIVE ADVICE

Now I admit that I have the advice disease pretty badly. When people come to me to talk something over, I look for suggestions, sometimes before they have finished explaining the background. If the topic is in my comfort zone I jump to an assumption about what they are about to say in no time and start planning my advice. OK, so if advice avalanche is a disease, what is the cure?

I tried out this technique with an old friend. He has written a number of successful radio plays but has been trying for a while now to write a stage play. From time to time he e-mails me the latest version of his script and asks for comments. Sometimes he asks for specific help on something that is holding him up. My normal method would be to read the script and then phone with fifteen suggestions. He then rejects half of them straight away and asks me to write down a couple of paras about the ones that remain. I do this, send it off and may not hear from him again for a while.

So, the last time this happened I decided to give him a thinking partnership and listen while he worked the problem out. The problem was simple: near the end of act one he had six characters on stage. He needed to reduce this to two for a short piece of dialogue that would set up the beginning of act two. He was having difficulties finding compelling reasons why the other four characters should leave the stage. The key problem was to invent an exit for Maggie and I asked the question, 'If you could get Maggie off the stage what would you do next?' The playwright thought out loud, long and hard; without doubt we had created a thinking environment. After a long time he had worked it out and knew how to lose three of the characters. 'But that still leaves Maggie', he moaned. At this point I cracked. We had been on the phone for about an hour and both my ears hurt. I simply gave out a torrent of ideas, or advice, about how to get Maggie off the bloody stage!

OK, I am not very good at it yet, but I could see the power of the exercise in helping the thinker to come to the best conclusion.

A lot of top people believe 'listening' to be a key career skill; see IDEA 34, *Don't talk so much*.

Try another idea...

Action is only as good as the thinking behind it. Thinking is only as good as the way people treat each other. A leader's job is to create an environment in which people can think for themselves and find the courage to put the best ideas into action.
PENNY FERGUSON, personal leadership guru

Defining idea...

How did it go?

Q **Look, I tried to cut down the amount of advice I gave to a team member recently and the meeting simply dried up. He explained that he was rather hoping that I would give him some advice. What should I have done?**

A *Sometimes, of course, it is totally appropriate to give advice; it's just that we tend to do it too often. Also, think about your questioning technique; most people continue to respond to good questions. Explain to people what you are doing and why, emphasising the development opportunity for them if they think and find the solution themselves.*

Q **Are you saying I should let someone go off on a route that I know will probably fail?**

A *I think I am, yes. If they are bright enough they will probably realise what is going to happen and change course. If they don't then, yes, people learn a lot from their mistakes. Anyone who never makes a mistake is not trying.*

Q **If I export all my best people won't I run the risk of not being able to meet my objectives and won't I spend all my time training people up?**

A *Hang on, how long are you thinking of staying in that job? Time your next promotion carefully.*

3

Make good suggestions loudly

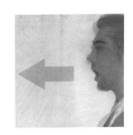

At any point in the chaos that describes your organisation, an opportunity can arise for you to make a sensible suggestion to the powers that be. Career people should grab such opportunities and actively seek them out.

The opportunities are legion. You've found an uncompetitive product feature, an outdated business process or an opportunity for new technology. Now's your chance to make sensible suggestions. Or think about publicity or sponsorship.

If you know the arts or sport preferences of the CEO, for example, you might just stumble across a local opportunity for sponsorship. If you make that happen, you can be sure the chief executive will be there for the event.

High-profile people get noticed, and the higher up the people doing the noticing the better. Form a plan for getting more than your fair share of senior management's attention, and then communicate your ideas clearly in a brief paper.

Here's an idea for you... **When did you last meet the most senior person in your building? If you are not based at the company's headquarters the answer to that question has to be at least in the last month. Take responsibility for this – do you know when you will next have an opportunity to meet senior people?**

First make sure that your idea is in an area where the issues are being discussed at least two levels above you. Now put up your paper.

You'll soon realise how vitally important it is that your boss thinks you are top-notch, and that you help to make him or her look brilliant as well. And not only your boss, but also your boss's boss.

MAKE SURE THEY CAN BEAR TO READ IT

So, you have a good idea. Now think about the quality of the communication. Think through, for example, the level of detail your boss wants to read and hear. As you go up the organisation you find people who are capable of going into detail, but less likely to want to. In both written and oral communications, write clear, simple management summaries.

Once you have written your paper, try to shorten it significantly, say by half. Throw out anything except the essentials. Remember you want to have the opportunity to discuss it. If it is too comprehensive you may have given the thing lock, stock and barrel for someone else to dine out on. Release it effectively – in other words in the way that best serves your interests. After all, it was your idea.

A good paper may help in other ways as well. There are lots of conferences out there, and lots of organisers looking for people to read papers. Reading a paper anywhere abroad, for example, looks good on the CV.

BE CREATIVE IN GETTING YOUR IDEAS TO THE RIGHT PEOPLE

To follow up your paper and for other reasons, there are many ways of communicating with the great and the good in your organisation

A paper on organisational change can be a good idea. Have a look at IDEA 10, *Don't leave your job behind when you move on.*

Try another idea...

outside the normal business environment. Volunteer for these. I don't mean volunteer for anything that has a low impact no matter how worthy. There is no point for the careerist in being a member of the St John's ambulance team at the local football ground. But there may be a point in being the fire officer for your floor. Check it out first. Does it get you in front of the Director of Logistics? Is there an opportunity to be a representative on the pension council? That's a high profile place.

Another promising area is promoting the company at sport by wearing the logo. If you are good at sport, senior managers will bask in your limelight. You will also come into contact with the people you are trying to impress if they come to the golf match you have arranged. Ask them to make a speech (and offer to help with some gags perhaps) and present the prizes.

Another good place to get your ideas known is the company newsletter, particularly if it involves interviewing senior people. Only speak at the Christmas party if you are really good at making people laugh. If being witty does not come naturally to you, speak at conferences where being amusing is a significant but secondary requirement.

'Think about the 4 C's, Continuous learning, Confidence in yourself, Care and attention to those you love and Communication – wherever you are, well-honed communication skills are highly important.'
Chairman, Scottish Power

Defining idea...

11

How did it go?

Q **I think I wrote quite a good paper and that it communicated the suggestion well. How can I be sure?**

A *There is only one real test of effective communication – did you meet the objective of the paper? Setting clear objectives and asking your audience if you have met them tells you if your communication has been effective. It may not have been elegant or hilarious, but did it do the job? A paper must end with some action points. If they happened, you communicated well.*

Q **Listen, mate, it's OK for you to make flashy suggestions about sport and sponsorship, but getting an idea like that can be dangerous. I decided to participate in the sponsorship of a major horse race. I got a good level of customer contact there, a senior manager from our lot pitched up and it was very well organised. Unfortunately, I went a bit over budget, but the event got such raves that nobody minded. This year I did it again but on a much more lavish scale. It was wildly successful but miles over budget. This time the finance people dumped on me from a great height; so thanks a bunch.**

A *Timing is all, as the comic said of the rhythm method. The time to really lash out on a lavish scale is as a last triumphant gesture before moving on to your next job. Don't do it when you have to stay behind and take the consequences.*

4

Don't come to me with your problems

When does a member of a team get their boss involved in a situation? Answer: when there's a problem.

Once you've made it to first- and second-line management the colleague competition has thinned out a bit — that's the good news. The bad news is that the real no-hopers have mostly disappeared and standing out in the smaller crowd is a bit more difficult.

All your competitors have, at some point, impressed senior people with their achievements or just their bonhomie and charisma. You need a career-friendly approach to working with your boss and getting his or her support.

HOUSTON, WE HAVE A PROBLEM

The best way to understand this idea is to think about second-line managers in the maintenance department of, say, a computer company. They actually only get involved with customers when all is far from well. They spend half their lives

13

Here's an
idea for
you...

Take the most difficult customer problem you have at the moment. Is it the right time to bring your boss in, or is it too early, or too late? Can you get nearer to the solution before you bring him or her in? Is it worth doing a SWOT analysis to see if you can come up with a solution?

talking to customers who are beside themselves with rage and threatening to write to the newspapers.

This 'there's a problem business' happens to all managers and it's pretty demoralising continuously to receive briefings that turn out to be problems. It may come as a surprise to a lot of people but their bosses do not automatically know what to do in all circumstances. It happens at all levels. I have known Chairmen and other senior managers still showing frustration at the way people present them with information in problem form.

CRISIS, WHAT CRISIS?

There are the three ways of telling your boss that there is a problem:

Take the piece of information (say, a competitor that has brought out a new product or a big customer who has gone bust) to your boss and wait for her to give you instructions.

Analyse your company's position in the light of the information. A very good way of doing this is to use simple SWOT analysis – strengths, weaknesses, opportunities and threats. What are the strengths that your company could use to combat the turn of events? What are the weaknesses that will make an effective response difficult? What opportunities does the new situation offer, and what are threats to performance if nothing is done? This is a much better approach as far as

Try
another
idea...

There's a bit on it being easier to ask for forgiveness rather than for permission in IDEA 9, What do you recommend?

your boss is concerned. It saves her time thinking the analysis through and makes it easier to make a decision. Watch your timing on this. If the problem is that a competitor has brought out a new product you have more time to weigh up the situation than if the customer has gone bust. But don't over-analyse and leave it too late to tell your boss. Having said that, most people err on the side of going in too quickly where more preparation would have been useful.

The business of getting from a good SWOT analysis to an equally good plan is more difficult than it appears in the first place. Try IDEA 38, *Draw your own map*.

Try another idea...

Using the SWOT analysis, come to a conclusion. Think through a well-structured line of reasoning that supports your recommendation and present the solution rather than the problem.

Most people take the first approach, some the second but only a few the third. Think about it from the point of view of the manager whose daily lot it is to receive a continuous stream of problems. The people who present the solutions really do stand out in the crowd.

FINALLY

The help that your 'solutions not problems' approach gives to your boss does have a downside. She may disagree with your solution, or know a better one from experience. But if you never make a mistake you are not trying to add value. It's all part of taking responsibility.

'What we're saying today is that you're either part of the solution or part of the problem.'
ELDRIDGE CLEAVER, American politician

Defining idea...

As one manager put it, 'The corporate world is made up of two types of person, those who play the game and those who watch it. You can tell them by what makes them feel good. The watcher goes home fulfilled if they have worked hard and used their skills. They have performed their tasks. The players only feel good if they have accomplished something. They finish things. They don't pass the buck. Funnily enough it is the players who make most mistakes. The watchers can't, because if you are not playing, you can't lose. Mind you, you can't win either.'

How did it go?

Q **I used your method to find the answer to a problem I was struggling with, and came to a pretty natty conclusion. I should just have done it, but I thought I'd better get top cover and took it to my boss. She then escalated the problem up the hierarchy and something I know could have been easily dealt with became a big issue. Wouldn't I have been better not to tell her anything and just gone ahead?**

A *Probably, yes. Getting top cover can be done after the event as well as before, if you see what I mean. Act first and then explain what you have done. You might work out some way to show that it was difficult or impossible to tell her beforehand as well. But don't get caught.*

Q **I took a solution to my boss but he jumped into action before I even had time to finish explaining it. He was on the phone starting to sort things out two minutes after I entered his office. How can I avoid this next time?**

A *You could try taking the most difficult issues to him after hours so that he can't use his phone. Perhaps you could tell him that you have started to implement your solution and just wanted to check your plan with him. Mmm, but he sounds a bit difficult. Don't come to me with your problems.*

5

Watch out for holiday surprises

In a cut-and-thrust environment where career people are jostling for position and influence, holidays can take on a sinister aspect. They offer two types of opportunity – people use them to be absent when something unpleasant is about to occur, and you can use the absence of others to get things done that otherwise wouldn't happen.

The first opportunity works like this. One of the salespeople who worked for me, we'll call him Jan, was managing a big campaign to sell a lot of computer equipment to a major local authority.

He was in competition with IBM, but had become increasingly confident that it was going his way.

The culmination of the campaign was to be a visit to the Chief Executive of the authority, with Jan, my boss and a director representing our company. Jan told me

Here's an idea for you... **Most people hate patent injustice in the workplace. It's worth taking another look at any incentive schemes you have in place and ask yourself if it's possible for someone to do everything wrong but still earn their bonuses and incentives. If it is, write something into the scheme to correct it. (Mind you, having said that, most of the people presiding over major collapses of big companies over the last few years seem to have looked after themselves pretty well.)**

that there was a good chance that we would get the order there and then. Suddenly with about a week to go, he announced that he was taking a short holiday and would miss this top-level meeting.

Stupidly I smelt no rat, took the opportunity of going to the meeting myself, and was there when the bombshell landed. They had, of course, decided to go with IBM and took this opportunity to inform us. It was, I think, the most embarrassing meeting of my business life. Actually, in the end my boss and I soon fixed things by making a huge price concession, and Jan came back with little to do except get the contracts signed and pick up his bonus.

So what had happened here? Jan had obviously seen the writing on the wall and decided that his presence in the ensuing mêlée would make little difference and be pretty painful; so he ducked out. In the end, though, the real fault was mine for not questioning why an ambitious man would give up high-level glory for a holiday. That's why I tell this story. Beware of the sudden holiday announcement. Incidentally, he might have got the bonus, but Jan became quickly aware that his career on my patch was mortally wounded and only worked for me for another two months.

Try another idea... **If you are negotiating an employment contract read IDEA 33, *Fail richly*.**

18

FIRING PEOPLE WITH FIRE

Perhaps the most famous incident of a manager taking advantage of another manager's absence on holiday is the case of John H. Patterson, the founder of NCR, and his sidekick of many years, Tom Watson Senior. Robertson decided that Watson was becoming a disruptive influence, probably true, and that there wasn't room in one company for both of them, certainly true. So, he purged head office of all the Watson cronies and fans when Watson was on holiday and uncontactable. The first Watson knew about it was on his return, when he found his desk, chair and effects on the lawn outside the office block – on fire. Ah, the technology pioneers of their day had style. Watson, of course, went off and founded IBM.

So, if powerful influencers are adversely affecting your position, use their time on holiday to bring their people into line and pull matters firmly in your direction. It is possibly also a good idea to stay in touch when you are on holiday yourself, but even in a book designed for the nakedly ambitious, I won't recommend that.

If you are looking for a slightly less dramatic way to fire someone, try IDEA 21, *Ready, aim, fire.*

Try another idea...

'*You are going to get a big surprise with the next thing I do.*'
DIANA, PRINCESS OF WALES

Defining idea...

How did it go?

Q **I have a situation where this idea could help very well. I want to buy a piece of equipment for my factory, but it's not on the list of recommended products put out by the production controller. Worse still, the supplier isn't on the list of recommended suppliers. I know when the controller is going on holiday and I think I will act then. I don't think the production director could care less, but should I tell him first?**

A *Good plan so far. Remember that it is always easier to ask for forgiveness rather than permission. Take care with the director. I would be inclined to write a note about it, copy it to him and then act immediately, perhaps before he's had a chance to read the note.*

Q **I used the absence of our finance controller on holiday to go to her boss and get agreement to an expenditure that I know she would have stopped. Does it matter that she has never really forgiven me?**

A *When I have got to someone's boss against their will, I have generally found that it doesn't matter. After all, the controller can't change the fact that you are in touch with her boss or that you've spent the money.*

6

Do you want to ride in the Derby or pull a coal cart?

Organisations serve their shareholders. Organisations also often include a mixture of businesses. Some are high risk with the potential of high return; others are lower risk and are expected to return lower profitability. Make sure your career's in the right one.

Who's in charge here? A bit of background first. A company exists to serve its shareholders, so it's best to take their requirements into account in planning your career. They are the people who believed in the company enough to put their money in it; but in the end they want a return.

You need to be thoroughly familiar with how shareholders regard companies. This may seem unnecessary at middle levels in the organisation, but your bit of the organisation is, after all, part of the whole.

Look at the risk of any plan or project you are proposing. Does it fit the risk profile of your division or organisation?

Shareholders choose investments based on, among other things, the level of risk involved. Someone speculating long term can afford to take on high-risk ventures. A retired person looking for relatively safe income will probably choose low risk. An important point here is that investors are not particularly keen on companies that are difficult to define in risk terms. As we'll see, this can enormously impact your career.

Any idea you take to your boss, particularly when you need the company to invest money, must in some way pay attention to both risk and return. If your scheme does not make money and generate cash at some point, it is not aimed at the heart of the company's purpose. OK, I know it's the bleedin' obvious, but you should see some of the fanciful proposals I've seen. Finally, you must predict that the return will come at an acceptable risk.

THINKING ABOUT RISK AND RETURN

Right, which bit of the business do you want to be in? Since you are career-oriented you would probably be best in that part of the business that is leading the field and making the most rapid progress. Ask yourself some key questions: where is growth happening, which division is most tied up with technology, where are the successful teams generating fame and fortune? If you are in that area already, look for opportunities to lead more growth. After all, it is the Derby.

If you are in the part of the business that's dragging the coal cart you are trying to be

'**Long range planning does not deal with future decisions. It deals with the futurity of present decisions.**'
PETER DRUCKER, management thinker and author

noticed in an area that people rarely bother to look at. It keeps delivering mundane profits and it provides good cash flows for the whizz-kids on the racehorses to speculate with; so senior managers are probably leaving well alone. There's another reason, too, for changing tack if you are in the cash cow. Think about the long-term fit of your division within the whole company – if they are looking to thrill the market they may sell your sort of business off or demerge it. In that way they can present a single risk profile to the shareholders rather than a confusing mixture.

Incidentally, if you are financially minded you can gauge the overall risk of your organisation by looking at the price/earnings ratio. If it's above, say, 20 it is an organisation that takes risks. If it is below 12 it probably doesn't much like high-risk projects.

If you are in the throes of planning a project look at IDEA 42, Nothing can go wrong...

Try another idea...

'It is just as easy to make a profit today as it will be tomorrow. Actions taken which result in reducing short-term profit in the hope of increasing long-term profit are very seldom successful. Such actions are almost always the result of wishful thinking and almost always fail to achieve an overall optimum performance.'
DAVID PACKARD, computer company founder

Defining idea...

23

How did
it go?

Q **When I go through the company's process of investment appraisal, I fill in the forms, including the cost/benefit analysis. My proposal then goes off to the financial controllers, who eventually return it with a thing called 'rate of return' attached and their comments on my risk assessment. It's difficult to find out what they actually do with my numbers or how the system works. Is it worth my going to the effort of trying to find out?**

A *Bloody right, pal. Otherwise you'll always risk being blindsided by the accountants. Give an accountant a cost/benefit analysis and he will produce the return on investment result that he first thought of. This means that he can kick your lovely proposal into the long grass with the stroke of a spreadsheet. Don't forget how you hire an accountant. You give them a simple arithmetical problem and ask them to work out the answer. You obviously don't hire the one who gets the calculation wrong; but you also don't hire the one who gets it right. You hire the one who says, 'What number did you have in mind?'*

Q   **You're right about risk. In my organisation you can't get investment proposals through the various committees unless they have spectacular returns. How do my colleague managers find these big-return projects? I am about to propose some investment in technology. If I want to propose anything like the return some people come up with, I would have to exaggerate the benefits hugely.**

A   *Look at the timescale of the project. Put the exaggerated benefits towards the end of the cost/benefit analysis and make sure you have moved on before that period arrives.*

Q   **Isn't that a bit dishonest?**

A   *You didn't ask me about honesty. You asked me how your colleagues find these high-return projects. And I've told you.*

7

Lead with style

The ultimate test of leadership is the top job. As you progress in that direction you need the people above you and the people below you to admire the way you go about leading your team.

Good senior managers can smell a well-motivated, happy team from a mile off. The team members exude confidence. They work hard and make sacrifices.

They display pride in their work and in their membership of what they honestly believe is the best bit of the organisation. Not only that, but everyone, including Human Resources, will know that people are queuing up to get into that team. How do you create this aura?

Some say leaders are born and cannot be created, and it's true that your basic ability to get on with people is, to some extent, your starting point for being a leader. But there are a number of leadership techniques that develop your natural ability to make things happen. Think about motivation – leadership is the skill of persuading people to

Here's an idea for you...

At your next team meeting take the role of chairman absolutely seriously on at least one important topic. Do not make any proposals for possible actions yourself or appear to support any particular view. Let the team decide what to do, summarise their plan, and thank them for their hard work and good thinking.

co-operate *willingly* to achieve results. The willingly is key: you cannot force motivation on people; they have to want to do a good job. Motivation occurs when people feel that they're able to make their very best contribution.

DO YOU TELL 'EM OR SELL 'EM?

Some people talk about 'push and pull' management styles. Push is the 'do what you are told' or autocratic method; pull is the consulting, democratic way of leading people. You need a combination of the two for different people and in different situations.

Mike Brearley, sometime captain of the England cricket team, was reckoned to have 'a degree in people'. Here's an example told by Bob Willis, a fast bowler in Brearley's side. Willis was involved in Brearley's occasional winding up of the swashbuckling Ian Botham. When he felt that he needed to ginger Botham up, Brearley would signal to Willis, to take a message to Botham: 'Mike says that you're bowling like a girl.' Pity the poor batsman who faced the next ball from a seething Botham. Willis concluded this story by saying that if the captain had used the same words with him it would have destroyed his confidence and had the opposite effect. Useful things, degrees in people.

Defining idea...

'You can play your role hands off if it works, but the opposite of hands off management is scruff of the neck management.'
ARTHUR WARD, a serial non-executive director of many companies

So, your team leadership style can range from giving simple directives to group discussion and consensus. If you tend too much towards giving directions you will, among other things, stifle the creativity of the team. That in turn reduces the number of times you will be able to take a good new idea to your boss. There is almost nothing that boosts a career more than being the first to make an innovative idea work and having it taken up by the rest of the company. Everybody will want to talk to you about it.

It is not generally good practice to show that you could do every team member's job better than them. We touch on this in IDEA 49, *Make your team your wings and soar.*

Try another idea...

FINALLY

Always remember that people work for money but will do a bit extra for recognition, praise and reward. If you think someone is doing a good job don't forget to tell them. Show appreciation often. Don't wait for the end of a task to say thanks. It is often a good idea to thank someone in the middle of a project for getting on with it without having to involve you.

So, show a genuine interest in other people, communicate well and pick the right style at the right time and you will probably become a born leader and smell beautiful to senior managers.

'It was the nation and the race dwelling all round the globe that had the lion's heart. I had the luck to be called upon to give the roar.'
WINSTON CHURCHILL

Defining idea...

Q **I tend to run my team with a vigorous push style and I have fallen into the trap of displaying the fact that I could do the job better than them. I have, after all, actually done all the jobs below me. I know that one of my guys is about to do something less than perfectly. What do I do? Just let him get on with it?**

A *Well yes, as long as it's not going to damage performance significantly. Let him do it his way. If it works in the end, what does it matter? If it goes wrong, he'll learn from the mistake. Eventually what will happen is that someone will do something differently to you and get a better result. You have to let the team develop if you want to smell of success.*

Q **I tried your idea about being the chair of a meeting and not making my views known. Next thing, the most senior member in the team takes over the proposing and leading role. How do you stop someone else stepping in to dominate proceedings?**

A *You could try briefing her on what you are trying to do before the event. If that doesn't work you must use what is called a 'labelled shut out'. You name the offender, and tell her you want to hear another named person out. Don't forget to bring the quietest members in to the discussion. You never know where the best ideas will come from.*

Q **This consensus stuff is for the birds. If the team is rushing around saying that they are coming up with all the ideas, won't I run the risk of looking like a weak leader?**

A *No, Adolf, you'll look like someone who gets the best out of their team.*

8

Actions speak louder than decisions

If you have taken a decision and informed your boss of what you and your team are going to do, for your career's sake make absolutely sure it happens.

If you haven't started the action plan, you may as well not have made a decision.

I've a friend who's an elderly painter and decorator. His children have moved on and he now has no dependents. He does not want to retire altogether but he does want to have more time for himself; but he's finding it difficult to cut down the amount of work he does. Unfortunately for him he is brilliant at his job and a very nice chap to boot. This means that his old clients all turn to him when they want work done and he finds it difficult to say no. Plus, his relatives and friends have been used to asking him over, giving him good food and drink and getting him to do some decorating.

Over coffee one day he asked me what I meant when I murmured that a decision is not a decision until there is commitment to the action plan and the first steps are taken. I asked him what he wanted to do in the spare time he was trying to create, and he rather coyly admitted that he had decided to take up golf. He then tried to implement his decision. He resolved to take every Friday off to pursue this new

Here's an idea for you...

Pick a team member who has difficulty with the 'do it now' concept. He tends to agree to a decision made by you, himself or the team, and then finds loads of reasons why he can't implement it. Sit him down and tell him the story of the painter. Now get him to take a decision he has been prevaricating over and put the actions into his diary. Phone him just before and just after he should have started to implement the decision.

hobby. Four weeks later he told me that he had not been able to do that once. I pressed him to commit to a lesson with the professional on the next Friday morning and another one that afternoon. We agreed that he would pay for the lessons in advance. This broke the deadlock and he started to play. He is now an addict and plays every Friday and quite often on other days as well – but it wasn't a decision until he'd gone into action.

Defining idea...

'Men of action whose minds are too busy with the day's work to see beyond it. They are essential men, we cannot do without them, and yet we must not allow all our vision to be bound by the limitations of men of action.'
PEARL S. BUCK, American writer

NEVER DISAPPOINT THE POWERS THAT BE

Right, where is this stuff important? Most teams work with some operational targets that they need urgently to achieve. If your team is well organised you'll also have a strategic plan that includes a series of projects aimed at improving the environment in which you operate. If you implement these projects, life will become easier and performance will improve. Being career-minded you will, of course, have told your boss all about the changes the team is going to make – perhaps with a loud drum roll. But in the real world pressure is always on maintaining performance rather than developing new methods. In my experience a boss will ask three times how you are getting on with the new idea. The third time they hear your excuse that unfortunately there just has not been time to get it going, they will forget it and write you down as all mouth and no trousers.

If you need to remind yourself about team strategy have a look at IDEA 18, _Don't play tennis with a cricket bat._

Try another idea...

'My choice in everything is to say nothing and go do it.'
LOU GERSTENER, American consultant and executive, CEO of IBM among others

Defining idea...

33

How did it go?

Q **Right, I got this bloke into my room and we discussed the fact that at our monthly team meetings he has never done any of the actions in the long-term plan. He could only agree and we put some very specific dates in his diary. He did them. Within a week or two major problems occurred on his patch. When I asked what had happened, he replied that he was following my instructions and so was busy with a new project as the storm gathered. That's why he had dropped the ball.**

A *You probably have a quite different problem here. If he deliberately turned his back knowing that issues would arise, he is sending a loud signal. Whatever he has said about the activities in the long-term plan, he does not believe that they are the right things to do or possibly that he has the skills and knowledge to do them. In other words he is not actually committed.*

Q **You're quite right about this.**

A *Thank you.*

Q **My team and I have so many half-started and half-finished bits and pieces lying around that they have lost interest in doing them at all, and I have lost credibility with my boss. How do I kick-start the important ones?**

Q *You've answered your own question. Go through the activities with the team, pick the important ones and throw all the others out. Sometimes when you are planning it is as vital to decide what not to do as it is to decide what to do.*

9

Know what to say to whom

A meteoric careerist can't have too much exposure to top people. Think hard about extending your senior contacts.

You happen to be in the lift with your Chairman, or a senior executive of a major customer. Make sure you know what you would say to them.

Most of us in such a situation are like rabbits caught in the headlights and blow this short window of time with small talk. There is a clue here for the careerist. But it's not just about the Chairman.

You can expand on this by dropping in on anyone. Hewlett Packard used to have a useful slogan, 'managing by wandering around'. It was a neat way of reminding managers that part of their job was to be around and meet people by chance as well as in formal meetings. I extended this to 'selling by wandering around', which meant using the same technique to cruise around customer premises making new, and preferably high-level, contacts. 'Cultivating your career by wandering around?' It's not as snappy but that doesn't mean that it doesn't work.

Here's an idea for you...

If, for example, you know your boss's diary you'll know when she is going to be talking to a person you would like to meet. First, prepare. If you did get the opportunity, what would you say? So, you know what you would say; now engineer the opportunity to say it. The best way is simply to breeze in. 'Oh, I'm sorry I didn't realise...' 'That's all right,' says your boss, 'Come in and meet Lord so-and-so.' She will probably add more in terms of a quick description of what you do for the organisation, and that is your moment. 'As a matter of fact, Lord so-and-so, I've been thinking that we ought to have a brief word on...' Brilliant: a new contact – put it in the address book.

PLAN YOUR ABSENCES

Try to be in the office at the same time as your boss. After all, in your absence she might give an interesting and potentially rewarding opportunity to someone else. You need to know her diary so that you can plan your absences at times when she won't notice you're not there.

The clincher for how vital it is to know your boss's diary is that you will know when she is definitely far away. Believe me, there is nothing more embarrassing than being caught nosing around in someone else's files.

Obviously you want high-level exposure to things that go well. You also want cover against being held responsible for something going wrong. Short-sighted people with moderate ambitions keep a detailed record of their activities with a note of the people who supported them on the way. The more ambitious person with her eye on the big picture does it in such a way that the record can prove that others were completely responsible if it goes wrong. Don't forget to have a shredder handy if all goes well, though. It wouldn't do for you to enable someone else to take the glory.

'It's not how you play the game, but who you get to take the blame' goes the rhyme. This is the business version of the Olympic spirit. If you're involved with high-level operations it's generally not a good idea to be closely associated with failure. Stay clear of the firing line unless there are massive Brownie points for effort as opposed to achievement.

What goes around comes around in business. IDEA 26, *What goes around comes around*, talks about the importance of keeping comprehensive personal records

Try another idea...

There is another way of looking at this if the cock-up is really huge. A person in charge of a substantial development project spent £50 million of his company's money on it and was, towards the end, powerless to prevent it having no impact on the business at all. The entire sum was completely wasted. Asked into his boss's office he pre-empted the inevitable by saying that he knew he was there to be fired. 'No way,' said his boss, a very aware woman, 'Now that we have spent £50 million on your learning what doesn't work, we are not about to throw that investment away.' It's a variant of the 'Owe your bank £1,000 it's your problem, owe it a million and it's theirs.'

'There is no stronger way of building a career than "working the corridors".'
RICHARD HUMPHREYS, serial chairman

Defining idea...

How did
it go?

Q **I made a new contact with the managing director of one of our key customers, went to see her and she loved an idea I put forward. She wants me to follow it through but there simply aren't enough hours in the day to do my job and this project.**

A *Nice one. Unless leaving your current position for a while would be dangerous, what about a secondment from your company to hers for the duration of the project. This looks brilliant on your CV and you are cultivating two careers at the same time.*

Q **People have noticed that I am always in when my boss is. It's not good to get a reputation as someone who sucks up is it?**

A *Tread a bit more subtly, squire. If you really are getting such a reputation it's probably more to do with how you talk to your boss and how heartily you laugh at his jokes than it is with always being there. A colleague of mine, Geoff, was a terrible crawler. Once he even came to a golf day, although he didn't play himself, and pulled his boss's golf trolley. At one hole the boss's ball went into the rough and his 'caddie' went streaking after it like a retriever. When he emerged from the woods there came a cry from nearby 'What does it taste like Geoff?'*

10

Don't leave your job behind when you move on

It is a great mistake in career planning to assume that the current management structure is the one in which you have to succeed. Indeed the opposite is the case, when you move on, your old job description should be obsolete; and it's also a good idea to create a new one.

Rock the boat! Many jobs exist because they have always done so, not because they represent the best way of getting things done.

If you go into a job and do things the best way possible, you'll probably find that the original job description bears no relationship to what you are doing. You get results, but when you move on your boss will have to change the structure and job description in line with how you got things done.

So use your influence and authority to get the best results possible without paying much attention to how things were done in the past. Most people just moan about the fact that 'they've got it all wrong', without attempting themselves to put it right. Again, the people who get to the top are the ones who take responsibility for their own actions. Keep saying to yourself that it is up to you.

Defining idea...

When Henry Lewis was the CEO of Marks & Spencer, he was asked why, out of all the management trainees that he joined with, he had made it right to the top said 'You know, I really have no idea.' After some thought he added, 'But I have noticed that every job I have ever done has been abolished after I left it.'

BE SUBTLE THEN SAVAGE – YOU WANT THE JOB

Don't just abolish your old job. Create your next one. Managers who succeed are the ones who help to prevent the organisation ossifying by suggesting new roles and responsibilities, one role being the next job they want.

Although it's easier to create a new job if the change will help the organisation achieve its objectives more effectively, it's possible to do it for purely selfish purposes. The creation of a new job is a two-part process. First, work out how to change the way of doing business so that the job has to exist. Now sell this idea. Show how the changes will benefit the business itself. If you reveal your hand at this stage there is a good chance that you are mistiming it by going too early. Don't give anyone the opportunity to say that what you are doing is for your own greater glory rather than the advancement of the organisation.

Having sold the change, produce your implementation plan and, of course, include the new positions required. Get everyone to agree the business benefits. Do not at this stage play the shrinking violet; clearly show that you are the person for the role you have chosen and defined. And tell people that you should have the job. Make sure the new job description has all the elements needed for the next step – access to senior management and a high profile when required. The risk and return on this career procedure will be very good if you have got it right. After all, you have moulded a job where the circumstances and your skills will be a perfect fit.

The annual appraisal might be the right occasion to abolish or create a job. Preparing well for this is a crucial part of cultivating your career. See IDEA 30, *You're totally responsible for you.*

Try another idea...

If you are really clever, or really lucky, creating a job can be a low-risk activity. Look for an opportunity where the business benefits would occur anyway, even if you went off on a cycling tour of Bolivia. From your inside knowledge you should be in the best position to understand this. An old Chinese proverb says, 'He who knows where the treasure is, needs no map.' Actually I just made that up, but you get the picture.

A President of RCA is reported to have answered the question 'Why, when so many were called were you chosen?' with the opposite of Henry Lewis's remark. He also purported not to know but said, 'I have noticed that no job I ever did existed before I got it.'

Defining idea...

How did it go?

Q Consultants or people from Human Resources are always thinking about the organisation and suggesting changes. How do I make my change work in the context of all of that?

A *Ignore them. What they are going to suggest won't work anyway. Keep with the business managers who actually have to bring in the results. If there is a clash between what you and your boss thinks needs to be done and what HR think, leave it to your boss to sort out the staffers.*

Q I loved the bit about creating your own job and designed a beauty. I put up a paper to my boss who loved it. Then the proposed new post had to go through some sort of job evaluation by a committee with a consultant on it. What do I do now it has come back at a grade less than the one I am already on?

A *Aha, that's foiled your little scheme. Try to find out how their evaluation system works. Then adjust the job description to fit a higher grade and persuade your boss to present it again. Either that or take the bastards on – 'You can't find a formula for grading a subtle senior management job in the same way as you can count the keystrokes of a data collector', and so on. Give your boss's boss the ammunition to bludgeon your idea through.*

11

How do I look?

Like it or not, your appearance and your health are of more and more interest to your employer. Think about what you look like and whether you are paying enough attention to fitness.

Are you fit for the purpose? It does, of course, depend. If your boss is a fitness freak you have a choice of two courses of action. Either you can join her and beat the hell out of your colleagues at squash or tennis or whatever, or you can religiously avoid exercise of all sorts. The latter makes a definite point, so think about it.

Nowadays there are myriad ways of keeping fit by working out before or after office hours. If you are a bit anti-exercise, which you probably are if you are reading this Idea, look carefully at all the opportunities. You don't have to do circuit training on a

Here's an idea for you...

It is never a good idea in career terms to fail at anything, so don't try and do too much. For example, try using a personal trainer just once a week or twice a month. That should spur you to some effort. It will eventually be embarrassing to tell them week after week that you haven't been off the sofa since you last met.

daily basis to give the impression that your health is as important to you as it is to your company. Walking can do it; so can cycling, jogging or roller-skating. If, however, your only exercise is straining to get the cork out of the bottle and the occasional one night stand, you could follow nutritionist Nigel Bentley's advice and get off the bus or the tube a few stops early and walk the rest of the way. If that doesn't suit you, try sitting on a horse. That's a fine way to get some fresh air, good exercise and, for goodness sake, a bit of excitement – you're quite high up off the ground. I've found that a bit of horse riding woke me up in the morning brilliantly and was as good a cure for a hangover as any.

If there are sports facilities at work use them by all means, but don't make a big thing about it. A lot of people, maybe most people, eventually find doing gym exercises monotonous and boring. So don't make yourself a hostage to fortune by shouting off about going to the gym every day after work; your bosses will notice when you stop.

A colleague of mine, Tony, tells the story of his personal trainer. Tony is a man who could eat for his country. He puts as much passion into eating and drinking as he does into his pretty successful career. The price he pays is a weight problem. At appraisal time his boss seemed to make light of it when he said 'What about shedding a bit of weight, Tony, we don't want to lose you to a heart attack.' Tony realised that there was more to the comment than light-hearted banter, so he hired a personal trainer. The woman took her job as a trainer very seriously and went through a detailed questionnaire on Tony's lifestyle and dietary habits. Each item was scored and at the end of the questions she totted up Tony's total, read the possible outcomes and finally announced in a puzzled voice that according to her charts he was already dead.

Incidentally if you're inclined to tell a personal trainer lies about your exercise regime, try reading the Robert Townsend quote in IDEA 1, *Face it, you are you and they are them.*

Try another idea...

WHAT DO YOUR CLOTHES SAY?

The advice of one of the senior telecommunications people I have trained is not for the faint hearted. He says that you should avoid looking like everyone else. If the first thing board members know about you is that you wear bow ties, you have made your point. Some of them may not like it, but this is compensated for by the fact that they've noticed you. I was always a little nervous about the topic of appearance in my one-on-one coaching sessions with senior managers. In the end I decided that the right question to ask yourself is whether your clothes are saying what you want them to say. Back to the telecommunications man. He always wore eccentric clothes – green corduroy suits featured heavily, along with brightly coloured braces and ties. In the nature of the training course I had to ask the question 'What do you think your clothes say about you?' He responded, 'They say that although I have got a senior job in your organisation, you will never own me.' I couldn't argue with that.

**'This is the Law of the Yukon, that only the Strong shall thrive;
That surely the Weak shall perish, and only the Fit survive.'**
ROBERT W. SERVICE, Canadian poet

Defining idea...

How did it go?

Q **I started to enjoy getting fit when they put a gym into the basement. But the people who do it tend to be the strong silent types and I've lost touch with a valuable grapevine I used to be plugged into. How do I keep up with, or in with, the people I used to gossip with in the pub after work?**

A *Ah, you are trying to run with the fox and ride with the hounds, an excellent idea in career terms. Never mind a foot in both camps, what you want is one in each tent. Take a night off the treadmill at least once a week for god's sake. You're trying to become Mr Chairman, not Mr Universe.*

Q **My boss looks like an unmade bed and emits a definite pong. You should see the funny looks he gets from our customers. Should I tell him?**

A *Noooo. It's much too dangerous. Get someone else to tell him. Probably best is your Human Resources contact, or if you are feeling brave, your boss's boss. Be warned: I once talked to a delegate about her appearance in a one-on-one coaching session. She took the hump with me and it did me no good at all.*

12

Please Sir, can I have some more?

Salary is an important component of your brilliant career. It also defines one of the main boundaries of your lifestyle. Negotiate for more when the time is ripe. Make sure you are being paid at least what you are worth and preferably a bit more.

NEVER tell anyone your salary. Whatever you say will do you or them no good. Either it will be less than they thought, which diminishes their respect, or it will be more than they either expect or think you are worth. This leads to jealousy.

Keep the big picture in view. Particularly at the start of your career, keep in mind that the rewards of getting to the top are very substantial. Don't whinge about your early salary. Tell yourself that you are investing for the future. Agree to small or no rises and even no promotions for the first couple of years, then go for the big hike when you have something to argue with.

Here's an idea for you... **By using recruitment agencies, the internet and the HR department you should be able to work out the top and bottom ends of the sort of salary someone in your position gets. Now work out why you deserve to be in the top 25% of the band. When you have a good case, take it to your boss. If you are already in the top quartile, look for a promotion.**

You might be better off doing an extra few months at 20k a year rather than causing grief by bellyaching. The eventual return could be well worth it.

I was working in a theatre once when an assistant stage manager did a bunk with the £100 she had been given to buy props. 'What a mug,' said a more seasoned ASM, 'If she had waited a bit longer she could have gone off with five times that.' So it is in business. It's only the people with no vision who fiddle their expenses for a couple of pints in the pub, or charge for a first-class train fare and sit in second. This is short sighted in many ways. After all, who do you need to impress who sits in standard class?

IT'S A LOT ABOUT TIMING

When you are going into a new job make sure that they really want you to join them and preferably have told other contenders that the job is not theirs before negotiating the salary. Asking earlier has two disadvantages. First, you may discover that there is a big gap between their expectations and yours. At that time you are negotiating from a position of weakness, since they have not yet decided if they want you. Second, it makes you look a bit small if the salary is the only reason you're taking the job.

Whatever anyone tells you, you can ask for more money at any time. The key here is timing: ask when your value to the organisation appears very high. Do it when you have just brought off a big deal, or organised the district conference or made a useful suggestion for change. Focus on what you have done and what you will do in the future. Use simple techniques of negotiation like the 'It's only 10 a week rather than 520 a year.'

If you are going for a very senior position you could try IDEA 33, _Fail rich._

Try another idea...

The same timing works when you're looking for a promotion. Think, act and look as though you are already in the new job. Seek out, and go after, vacancies. I was managing a small sales team in Scotland when the manager of a large team in a higher job category got a promotion. As soon as I heard the news I telephoned his boss, whom I knew, and asked for the job. I think he was simply saving the time and stress of interviewing when he agreed.

'The salary of the Chief Executive of the large corporation is not a market reward for achievement. It is frequently in the nature of a warm personal gesture from the person to him or her self.'
J.K. GALBRAITH, American economist

Defining idea...

49

Q **Is it possible to get over the company policy that salaries are only reviewed once a year?**

A *Normally yes, and certainly in very many cases. If you've increased your worth over the last twelve months, combine this enhanced status with a hint of unfairness. In terms of unfairness it is probably best to avoid the straight 'But they're earning more than me.' Do it more subtly.*

Q **I think I am underpaid and am going to look for a new job if they don't do something about it. Should I tell them?**

A *If you use it as a gun to their head, you reduce the value equation and represent only a threat. It's generally not good news. The boldest way would be to get another job and then tell them that you have a real intention to move if they don't come up with the goods.*

13

Go on, give them a shock

As part of your campaign to gain high exposure to senior people, take any opportunity you can to introduce new information into the organisation.

Look at your organisation as though you were the owner.

Left to itself a company ossifies. All organisations need alert managers to tell them how the world in which they are operating is changing. And it is difficult to be sure what changes in the environment will have an impact on your particular organisation. This makes the gathering and proclaiming of new facts or statistics a fertile ground for standing out in the crowd. The aim here is to draw the attention of management to new information that might have a long-term impact. This is an area for lateral thinking. Remember, we are talking about the long term – you should be long gone by the time your predictions face a reality check.

Brilliant entrepreneurs do this stuff really well. They take, for example, something a customer said to them the other day, a project they just approved in research and development, something their teenage son said at breakfast together with a headline in today's paper and discover an insight. That's what you are trying to do here, develop the way of thinking that entrepreneurs use to plan the way ahead.

Here's an idea for you...

Look for external sources of information that senior manager will find useful. Customers and competitors are very fertile ground. Spend a bit of time today looking at information about a competitor. If you are financially inclined, compare your competitor's annual report with yours and look for major discrepancies. Now see if you can get your boss interested in going further into it.

Defining idea...

'Study your subject well; observe carefully your customer requirements; strive mightily to fulfil that customer need and work hard and diligently at all times.'
SIR GEORGE BULL, Chairman, J. Sainsbury

Make sure you set aside at least fifteen minutes of every day to read relevant published material; you will find this invaluable in presenting yourself. Reading technical papers, or even just the dailies, will help you to start to detect new and useful facts at an early stage. A rich vein for this type of information is the technical section. Technological change over the last ten years has rendered hundreds of traditional skills unnecessary. When, for example, did you last see someone literally cutting and pasting a newsletter?

LOOK FOR TRENDS, SOCIOLOGICAL AND OTHER

Send notes to appropriate people quoting sources of information such as the *Harvard Gazette* that no one is likely to have read. The conclusion that you draw from the information must give senior managers food for thought. You must lead them to some clear conclusions showing problems, preferably catastrophic ones, or opportunities, preferably big ones, in the future. The area of demographics is another dead cert. Grey people buying power, the growth of old retired people, the death rate in Russia and so on. I advocate strongly the use of real facts in this regard, but if you have to make them up make sure it is not remotely possible to challenge them.

If all else fails there is always regulation and health and safety. Find out the trends here and predict the impact on your organisation.

Gather new facts and statistics as often as seems sensible given that you are also over-performing in your day-to-day function, and you will almost certainly at some point do your organisation a big favour. It would have ossified in that area if you hadn't warned it: organisations don't spot trends. Sometimes, if the coming event is catastrophic, what you say will give them the most tremendous shock.

Health warning: Do not pull the facts and statistics stunt too often. Some people send off two notes a week. This is a mistake. You are trying to build a reputation as a person with their finger on the pulse, not as a crashing bore.

For more on this look at IDEA 4, ***Don't come to me with your problems.***

Try another idea...

'War is 90% information.'
NAPOLEON BONAPARTE

Defining idea...

53

How did it go?

Q **I found a section in a technical paper that will have a very significant impact on my company. I wrote it up and circulated it widely. I have now been asked to carry out a project to examine the possible impact and to suggest what actions we should take. It's a staff job. Should I be concerned that line managers might forget me if I do it?**

A *Brilliant, a great opportunity. Accept the post with alacrity, but make sure it has a strictly limited time frame. Discuss where you might go back into the field afterwards and ensure that the job description includes a lot of exposure to the line. That way they can't forget you.*

Q **I took your idea about researching the competition and went to my boss with a cautionary tale about their new products against ours. She accused me of being very negative and believing that the glass was half empty rather than half full. What did I do wrong?**

A *You didn't finish with a positive spin. Always present solutions rather than problems. You should've done a bit more analysis and come up with ways round the problem.*

14

Send an inside salesperson

Your CV is a selling document and the product it is selling is you. You want someone who is trying to fill a new post to reach for your CV and like what they see.

Get your CV out there: good salespeople cultivate an 'inside salesman', a sort of guardian angel that supports them and advances their case when they are not there. A CV can do the same thing for a person seeking a job or looking for promotion.

Nowadays it is very easy for the presentation of a CV to be first class, so anything else is a career suicide note. Make sure it is also in pristine condition every time.

I knew an aged actor of the old school. A stereotypical thesp, he had a booming voice that made every phrase sound as if it were by Shakespeare; and he was frequently out of work and so always short of money. He used to go around the local shops and cafés trying to cash cheques. One day he tried four or five places and got four or five polite refusals from shopkeepers who knew him. By this time the cheque look somewhat crumpled and dilapidated. His final try was at the

Here's an idea for you...

Keep application forms consistent and remember that different organisations are looking for different things. A young relative of mine was applying for her first job after university. Although she wasn't certain that a career in journalism was right for her, she had decided to apply for a trainee job at a newspaper publisher. To the question, 'What newspapers and periodicals do you regularly read?' she had replied confidently, and honestly, 'None.' Check that the information you give doesn't fly in the face of the type of post you are going for.

and another idea...

Once you have written your CV get as many people as possible to look it over for you. Take it to business managers who hire people into their teams and to someone who works in Human Resources. In the end the same document has to work for both.

laundry. 'Would you be so good as to cash me a small cheque?' he asked, 'I'm sorry,' came the reply, 'But we still have an old one of yours that bounced.' 'Oh well,' said the actor 'Could you at least iron the bloody thing?'

I was looking through a pile of CVs for a client recently and found one that looked just like that old actor's cheque, tatty and frequently presented. It was difficult for us to take the candidate seriously. CVs are silently selling or unselling you when you are not there.

How complete your CV is up to you, but you do not have to put anything on it that may damage your case. You can probably miss out the wrong job that only lasted six months, and a slight exaggeration of your role in your present company may help your chances of getting a more senior job with a competitor. Make the document fit the style of the job – formal and professional for the accountants, witty and outrageous for creative jobs.

OH WHAT A TANGLED WEB WE WEAVE, WHEN FIRST WE PRACTICE TO DECEIVE

Don't lie on your CV. Suppose a headhunter contacts you, always a flattering event, and you decide the job is pretty much what you are looking for. As you talk about your CV, you realise that the head-hunter has made an assumption that is not true. He thinks you were the project manager while actually you were the deputy. It is difficult, but almost certainly better, to put him right there and then, if only because he might find out later.

The chance of getting caught out is probably high enough for you to decide to tell the truth and nothing but the truth, but nobody said you had to tell the whole truth. People who lie at a promotion panel find that their biggest enemy is their body language. An experienced HR person can tell instantly when you are feeling uncomfortable.

Research shows that a quarter of all CVs contain lies. Most firms do not test for skills, so it is possible – though dangerous – to get away with an exaggeration of your computer or other skills. The humiliation when your boss uncovers your deception will give you a very rough start. A lie never ceases to be a ticking time bomb, and it's so easy to forget what you said if it wasn't the truth.

If the job seems ideal for you, and you seem ideal for the job, don't pretend to meet a criterion set by the employer; rather work out in your preparation why the criterion is unnecessary and/or how quickly you could become able to fulfil it in any case.

Your communication skills are a vital part of career cultivation. Have a look at IDEA 31, *Make them agree, fast.*

Try another idea...

'*Unless one is a genius, it is best to aim at being intelligible.*'
SIR ANTHONY HOPE HOPKINS, novelist

Defining idea...

How did it go?

Q **Look, I've written a brilliant CV and presented it beautifully. Then along comes their application form and I have to handwrite it. My terrible handwriting has made my application form look as though it were written by a ten year old. Any tips?**

A *Mmm, interesting one. Maybe ask the company to send you the document in Word or other form by e-mail so that you can fill it in electronically. Possibly scan it in? You could pray that this company doesn't use graphologists and get someone else with copperplate style to write it for you; but be ready to volunteer the fact that it is another person's work at the first hint of discovery.*

Q **I am trying to recruit a new member of the team. One guy has sent in exactly the sort of unprofessional document you describe. Do I obey my instincts and throw it away or look hard at the logic within the CV that says he has exactly the right experience?**

A *Go for the logic. It is probably easier to instil a more professional approach in the person with the right background than it is to train someone else who happens to be very organised, neat and tidy but lacks the real skills for the job.*

15

Back the right horse

You need to get noticed. Identify who is important to your progress, and get to them. Sometimes that will mean bypassing a human blockage – perhaps your own boss, or some obstructive gatekeeper who is there to keep you away from the decision maker. Here are some tactics to leap such hurdles.

Suppose, for example, that your job is to supply computer and telecommunications solutions to the finance department of your company.

Your customer and decision maker is the Finance Director, but on a day-to-day basis there will be a key person whom you meet regularly and with whom you form plans for future approval by the Finance Director. Such people can usually be divided into three categories – the Good, the Bad and the Ugly.

The Good are terrific to work with. They understand their business and they are happy to tell you all about it, so that you can come up with the best possible plan together. Cultivate such people. Latch on to their coat tails. Buy them lunch. Feign interest when they show you pictures of their family. Help them to enhance their reputations and they will help you enhance yours. They will probably be quite happy for you to talk to the ultimate decision maker should you need to, but they'll do it with you as part of the team.

Here's an idea for you...

Never ask Mr Bad for permission to go and see the decision maker. If he refuses (which he probably will), you're then in an impossible situation. If you go behind his back, then you're heading for a confrontation and the relationship will be ruined for good. No – do it first and beg forgiveness later.

The Bad are often bad because they are scared. They're scared of their boss, they're scared of making mistakes and they're probably scared of a brilliant careerist like you. They probably don't know enough about their business to really brief you on what it is they want and will probably bar you from seeing the decision maker until you have earned their trust. That is the vital element of dealing with the Bad – you have to gain their trust.

It should be quite easy for a cool careerist like you to do this. Achieve some good, high-profile results that end up on the Finance Director's desk, and make sure Mr Bad gets all the credit. But do this genuinely. If you have to, you can dump on him later by showing that it has been you and your team all along that got the results, but life is easier if you can avoid having to do this.

At the point when he trusts you, Mr Bad should let you meet his boss. There is a problem if he won't. Access to his Director is vital if you are to carry out your role. So, like it or not, you have to get to them.

Remember, 'it is much easier to ask for forgiveness than to ask for permission.' Once you have created a relationship with his boss, Mr Bad will never be in such a strong position again to get in your way.

Now for Mr Ugly. Mr Ugly is mean. He doesn't trust you, he doesn't trust his boss, he doesn't trust anyone. Quite often such people are bullies. You can't really play along with them if they are not allowing you to do the best you can for your customer; so you have to grasp the nettle and probably cause a major stink. Funnily enough, the way to deal with them is to cause them some fear, uncertainty and doubt.

It can be a good career move to work for an ugly manager. Have a look at IDEA 41, *Try working for a nineteenth-century mill owner.*

Try another idea...

DEALING WITH MR UGLY

One of my salespeople had a Mr Ugly to contend with. I had to go in to see him and explain very logically that if my salesperson could not see the boss I would have to go in myself. I then displayed knowledge of what this bloke's competitors were doing and showed him that he was losing ground by not investing enough with us. I kept him just short of blowing his top and his uncertainty made him a bit easier to deal with. Unfortunately, however, he would not keep up with technological change and buy a 2960 B from us.

He would not even talk about it. The time had come to take a big risk. We made an appointment to go and see the Director, his boss, and we specifically asked that the meeting be with him on his own. As we had hoped, the director knew there was something wrong in that part of his business and agreed, albeit with at least a show of reluctance. We were pretty nervous; this was a major knifing job on a fairly senior person in a big customer. The Director's opening was 'Now just before we get to the intriguing question of why you wanted to see me without Rob, I thought I better let you know that he has just recommended that we buy a 2960 B.'

'It is better to be beautiful than to be good. But...it is better to be good than to be ugly.'
OSCAR WILDE

Defining idea...

Q. **I have a product manager who, by your definition, is ugly. She has told me that she will arrange for my career to end if I so much as think about going to see her boss. There are some circumstances where you simply can't ignore a threat like this aren't there?**

A. *No.*

Q. **Any ways of doing it apart from taking a huge risk of aggressive retaliation?**

A. *Probably. The best way might be to come down the way to the decision maker. Work out how you can get the decision maker's boss to tell them to meet you. That way when Ms Ugly gets to know, you can just say that you were actually invited in to meet her boss. Alternatively, can you get to her boss at a social event or a conference or something like that?*

Q. **I don't like it – this woman is evil.**

A. *Ah, come on. Nobody said having a cool career was easy.*

16

Try working for a nineteenth-century mill owner

Some managers are just plain bastards. They are renowned for it and most people try to avoid them. Only work for them if the pay is better, or if it helps your brilliant career.

Some folk just can't do the interpersonal skills bit.

One of these people, a production director, was instructing a friend of mine to bulldoze his project through by making people co-operate. 'I don't care if you make yourself the most unpopular person in the company,' he declared. My friend, who had had enough, explained that that was impossible since the production director already held that position.

I survived one such boss who even gave me a thorough dressing down in front of her mother. Perhaps that demonstrated her problem. I mean if you have to show off in front of your mum when you are in your forties there's something wrong. I got promoted out of her team. I remember meeting my successor in the car park. He was looking crestfallen and I asked why. 'Her car is in the car park,' he said, 'so she's not only mad, but she's in the office.' 'Remind her to take her medication,' I

Here's an idea for you...

When you work for someone like this you will frequently find yourself listening to people slagging them off. The easy thing to do is to throw in your lot with them and get it all off your chest. Your brilliant career, however, demands the opposite approach. Suggest that people misunderstand your boss and that he or she is a talented person with, deep down, a heart of gold. Senior managers will appreciate how you defend your boss, your peers will start to suspect that they might be missing something and everyone will respect your loyalty. Managers notice any disloyalty and will remember it if they ever come to thinking about inviting you to work for them.

suggested helpfully. To this day I have wondered whether he did remind her, and also whether she actually took medication.

There are always opportunities where there are problems. If a manager has a reputation for being hard to work for and is generally unpopular, joining him or her may be exactly the right thing to do to. There are a number of possible outcomes:

If he or she is successful, then you can paint yourself as the person who calmed the troubled waters and made success possible.

If he or she is unsuccessful everyone will understand that it was not your fault, and you will be left in charge when they leave.

If the two of you fall apart, you may just be able to get some brownie points for trying.

KEEPING THE PEACE

I once worked for a fiery project manager who walked roughshod over anyone he believed was endangering his project. He had a fine line in abuse, and never held back from using it. I developed a good relationship with him and managed to tone down a lot of the vitriol he flung around the company. I also worked hard on my relationship with his boss's secretary, and she and I spoke often about smoothing off the rough edges of his direct approach. Between us we held the fort for about a year, until even we were powerless against a particularly vicious attack on a manager who was supporting an idea that happened to be the brainchild of the managing director. My man left, and I took his job on an interim basis despite my being very junior for it. I also, modestly, accepted the congratulations of his boss for having kept the man's talented contribution going for so long.

You are trying to become the friendly face in your boss's office. Have a look at IDEA 24, *Taking over a happy ship*.

Try another idea...

'To know all is not to forgive all. It is to despise everyone.'
QUENTIN CRISP

Defining idea...

Q. **I've got a boss just like that. The trouble is that slowly but surely I am becoming tarred with the same brush. Will people become wary of me and treat me as though I were he?**

A. *One thing you may be doing, you must stop. It sounds as though people think that the rough stuff is coming from you as well as him. Preface all communications with words such as 'Bob has asked me to give you this message', or 'I think Bob wants it done this way.' It's a fine line between dissasociating yourself from the bad ideas and hostile presentation of your boss (good), and being seen to be disloyal (bad).*

Q. **My boss is pretty universally hated. I'm using your idea about not being disloyal, but it's starting to wear thin. People are more challenging about him and I am starting to lose co-operation from some people because they don't want to do anything that might help him. Has it come to the point where I should just stab him firmly in the back and move on?**

A. *Hang on a minute. You must feel that he can help your career in some way or you would've done that ages ago. If that is the case, then you could try the really hard option and talk to him about it. Find some way of saying that he is losing the assistance of people who are essential to his performance as a manager or to his career. Human Resources might be able to help by suggesting some sort of interpersonal skills training.*

17

Encourage the musician in everyone

One of the best things you can do for your career is to deliver projects to your boss on time and within budget. Your team will deliver when you lead it effectively. Pick the right management style for the right situation.

There is a spectrum of leadership styles, and you will need to adopt them all at certain points in your working life. Your style will vary from autocratic 'do as I say' to democratic 'consensus-seeking'.

Your predominant style will depend on your organisation, the nature of the project and the characteristics of the team. Try not to make it too dependent on your natural way of leading people. You need to develop more flexibility than that.

You need to show your boss that you do not just hire people who are like yourself, but can manage anyone who you need in your team.

Here's an idea for you...

If you can't admit that you can't do something, your people won't either. Encourage them to talk about those parts of your strategy they are less confident of handling. Then you can help them, or rearrange the plan to take that task away from them. I have seen teams thrash out a good strategy, but plainly lack the skills to achieve it. I have even sat with senior managers who were brought in for the final presentation of the plan, and when the team has left the room they have turned to me and said 'Great plan, Ken, but that lot can't do it.' It begs the question, 'Why are you letting them try?'

Try another idea...

The importance of selling yourself high and wide is discussed in IDEA 9, *Know what to say to whom*.

Consider the appropriate times to use these different styles. Obviously when the project hits a crisis and there is no time to consult you'll have to make decisions alone, take the risks yourself and seize control. You will get through the crisis, but at the cost of teamwork. Try to use this style sparingly and remember that such heavy 'push' management tends to get results rapidly but its impact falls off just as quickly. If you want a change in performance to stick, you need to move along the spectrum towards consensus.

Opinion seeking is further along the spectrum. Ask all the stakeholders as well as your team what they think about a wide range of issues. This 'pull' type of management builds confidence and demonstrates that you value the team's views. It is also an opportunity to go high up in the organisation to get the advice of some senior people whose experience you would like to exploit. Stakeholders love it and it spreads the risk a bit if something goes wrong.

Finally you get to the truly democratic style of management. It is essential to use this style on a regular basis. It 'empowers' the team. (Am I the only person who thinks that the buzzword 'empower' is just good, old-fashioned trust dressed up to sound impressive?) Simply encourage team participation and involve them in making decisions. Keep them up to date with your thinking and with issues that are affecting the project. There is no doubt that people blossom under such a regime; they improve and maintain performance and motivation. They also speak well of you to your boss.

DEVELOP GOOD TEAM MEMBERS

In most teams the egos of the individuals can get in the way of sharing suggestions. There are exceptions and they tend to be successful people. Hire them. They encourage openness and constructive criticism of everyone, by everyone. They tend to be laid back, good listeners and understanding of people's problems. They are terrific allies of the team leader and still liked by their colleagues in the team. As team leaders themselves they bring the best out of people. They don't manage everyone in the same way, though. Some of the team they can encourage to be musicians, and some will always be actors.

Defining idea...

'*The function that distinguishes a manager above all others is his educational one. The one contribution he is uniquely expected to make is to give others vision and ability to perform. It is vision and more responsibility that, in the last analysis, define the manager.*'
PETER DRUCKER, creator of modern management theory

Defining idea...

'*Striking amongst the musicians is their total lack of self-importance. They play a piece and then discuss among themselves as to how it may be improved. They make suggestions for each other directly, not via the director. No actor would tolerate a fellow performer who ventured to comment on what he or she is doing – comment of that sort coming solely from the director, and even then it has to be carefully packaged and seasoned with plenty of love and appreciation.*'
ALAN BENNETT

69

How did it go?

Q. **I had a big decision to make and I had just read this stupid idea. Do you know how long it takes to make a decision if everyone has a say?**

A. *Ah, courage mon brave. They will get quicker at it and the time you lose in the meeting will be paid back because you have made the best decision and have a bunch of people motivated to implement it.*

Q. **My boss doesn't really like me adopting a consultative style. He wonders aloud why I don't just tell them what to do. When he sees me and the team trooping into a conference room he is prone to shout 'Ah, Ian, off for another wanktank?' How can I bring him on board?**

A. *Mmm, tricky, you are right to be concerned because if he loses it and just tells you to stop doing it you'll have a discontented team on your hands besides looking rather silly. You need a result with something in it for him. Talk to him about his big issues, discuss possible solutions in your next team meeting and see if you can't come up with an insight that even he has to grudgingly admit is helpful. But good luck. It is difficult to work with a boss who doesn't like your style.*

18

Find out what you are supposed to be doing

Your career depends on your organisation meeting its objectives, and your being widely seen as making a big contribution to those aims. Find out precisely what the organisation is trying to do before you work out your detailed plans.

Your career needs a winning plan of campaign that is on the same wavelength as your organisation's. Good careerists are better at planning than most people and they generally make sure they thoroughly understand their organisation's strategy before they craft their own.

The word 'strategy' is possibly the most ill-used piece of management speak in the business. Middle managers often complain that their board of directors doesn't have a strategy. This is normally not the case. The board's strategy may be wrong but it does have one. Maybe middle management has not been told about it or maybe they have misunderstood it. It is, in fact, a crucial function of the board to

Here's an idea for you... **OK, now we have agreed what a strategy is, get yourself a good definition of the strategy of any staff departments that are important to you. The marketing department is a good place to start – after all, they are responsible for agreeing the top-level strategy of what you are going to sell and to whom.**

plan and implement a strategy, so you need a reputation as a strategic thinker to get to the top. Memo to self: Start working on that now.

Come down a few levels to team leaders and the accusation that they don't have a strategy can look truer. It is difficult for them to have an up-to-date strategy, particularly in organisations that do not give concrete guidelines on what a strategy is and how and when to review it. Difficulties abound:

- It is difficult for a team leader to build a strategy because it takes time.

- Short-term pressures stop the team getting on with the job of creating a strategy and even when it does, the strategy is frequently ignored whenever a customer or other significant pressure blows it off course.

- Your best strategy may be impossible because other parts of the business will not change to suit you.

- Building a team strategy needs consensus, so some team members are going to have to compromise – never easy.

But if it's difficult it must be an area where the ambitious manager can build some career points. Put simply, you need to build a strategy with your team, agree it with all your main stakeholders or interested parties, including your customers, and flaunt it. But you've got to know the organisation's strategy before you start.

KEEP IT STRATEGICALLY SIMPLE, STUPID

To work out your organisation's strategy it's useful to start with what it's not:

- The annual budgeting round. Don't mistake this for strategy. You come to the budgeting activities when the rest of the strategy is worked out.

- A large book of management-speak containing mission statements of 400 words that attempt to cover all the aspirations of the management team without pausing for breath. Here is one of these at board level...

'Our strategic intent is to strive for leadership in the most attractive global communications segments through speed in anticipating and fulfilling evolving customer needs, quality in products and processes, as well as openness with people and to new ideas and solutions. Based on our resources including technological know-how, market position and continuous building of competencies, we are well positioned to achieve our future goals.'

'Yes, but what are you going to *do*?' you long to scream.

Try another idea...

If you are happy that you know your organisation's strategy and want to start to build your own, go to IDEA 38, *Draw your own map.*

Defining idea...

'**A strategy is no good unless people fundamentally believe in it.**'
ROBERT HASS, businessman

A mission statement like that always reminds me of the old limerick:

There was a young man from Milan,
Whose limericks never would scan,
When his friends asked him why,
He said with a sigh,
'It's because I always try to put as many words into the last line as I possibly can.'

Back to what a strategy is not:

- A document produced by a staff function, carried around only by the same people, who use it solely to demonstrate that what the line departments are doing is against the strategy.

- A matrix of numbers produced once a year and left on the shelf until such time as it is due for review.

Right, keep it simple, what is it? A strategy is a plan of what an organisation is going to sell to which markets and how. The strategic plan allows everyone to know how they should do their jobs, what the boundaries are and how the board will appraise any suggestions for doing new things. It is the strategy's job to bring focus to everyone's work. You must get to know it in terms that are not business school babble.

From now on when someone complains that the board does not have a strategy, confidently ask him or her to explain, 'What exactly do you mean by a strategy?' You will be amazed at the number who can't or who give you a line from a limerick.

Q   **I asked the marketing folk what the strategy is and, guess what, I couldn't make head or tail of their reply. It included words like 'paradigm' and more 'models' than a *Playboy* shoot. Who's got it wrong, them or me?**

How did it go?

A   *Ah, at a guess, them; but you probably asked the wrong question. Try three: 'What products or services do we sell?' 'To whom do we sell them?' 'How do we go about doing the selling?' If this doesn't work try a line manager with the same set of questions.*

Q   **How can I try the idea with a marketing man who says that the strategy is company confidential and that he couldn't tell me it?**

A   *This man is an imbecile or mad or both. Go and talk to someone sensible and shop him.*

Q   **OK I did it. Then, once I understood the organisation's strategy, I got the team together, and it became obvious that one area in our department is going to become much less important than it was. How do I pick up the morale of the people involved in that area of the business?**

A   *First of all, well done. The issue is out in the open and you can start to deal with it. Have you made absolutely sure that they are convinced that their jobs are going to become marginalized or even cease to exist? Can the people retrain for the area that is growing? If the answer to both these questions is no, then you've got a problem. The people are not going to try to change, and if they were to try you don't think they can make it. Is there some way you can generously offload this part of your operation to someone else?*

19

You are totally responsible for you

It is a great mistake to think that anyone is as interested in your career as you are. Once you are past first-line management, you have to work out where you want to go and how to get there. Use the annual appraisal to get your boss's agreement to what you want to do.

Give your boss an easy time.

Even if you have a very open relationship with your boss the annual appraisal is vital to your career plan. Do the preparation and preferably do it better than your boss. No one is as dedicated to your career as you. No one is as good as you at knowing what skills you need. Help your boss along by working all that out before the appraisal interview.

Get yourself ready and in the right frame of mind by asking yourself these questions:

- What value have you added to your job?
- Where is it that you would like to go?
- What do you need to do to get there?
- Why should your boss support these plans? What's in it for her?

Here's an idea for you...

Lots of managers like to broadcast the fact that they don't really take the appraisal system seriously, that they have done no prep and that the whole thing will be over in twenty minutes. Encourage this thinking, agree that it's a ritual and that only the salary review has any significance. And then go home and do the preparation assiduously.

Answering these questions before an appraisal interview will mean that you will make the most productive use of this great opportunity to talk about yourself. Remember, this is your career, not your organisation's. Take ownership of that career and impress your boss with your motivation and determination. If you've got a clear idea of your career strategy you'll be much more impressive than an employee who agrees to whatever is suggested and has no proposals of his or her own. More or less writing your own appraisal should make life easier for your boss as well.

SELL THEM ON YOUR IDEAS FOR YOUR CAREER

While your career is your own, remember also that you are a team player in an organisation with its own aims and strategies. It is an entity in its own right and this must be reflected in the way you express yourself during an appraisal interview. That is why the question 'why should your boss support these plans?' is so important. You need to be able to prove that you are a valuable asset to the organisation and that if it invests in you, you will become even more valuable. Start from the very top. What words can you use that link your activities with the fundamental vision or mission of the organisation you work for? Then come down through the division and eventually to your boss.

Another key thing to remember at appraisal time is that the person interviewing you is not an unidentifiable member of the corporate zoo; she is in fact a person with her own ambitions and career plans. Be sensitive to this. Do not alienate your boss by appearing to be more ambitious, more clued up, more prepared to succeed than her (even if it's true). What you are trying to do is to get your boss to adopt your plan, which you present subtly and sensitively, because she can see how it is going to make her look good. You do not need to ram this down her throat; she can work it out.

Some managers are genuinely hated round the organisation. There can be a huge benefit in including them among the people you want to go to work for. See IDEA 16, *Try working for a nineteenth-century mill owner.*

Try another idea...

A little flattery can go along way. If you're feeling particularly outrageous, you could even suggest that one day you hope to attain the giddy heights of responsibility that your boss has (although this one takes a firm jaw, a straight face and a very sincere stance to get away with it).

You may already have a job purpose statement or job description agreed with your employer. If not, the appraisal is a splendid opportunity to define your own. If you already have a job purpose statement, expand on it to ensure that your future career aspirations are as easy as possible to achieve.

'Always take every opportunity offered to receive training. Give careful thought to your training needs before any appraisal interview.'
GEORGE PAUL, Chairman, Norwich Union

Defining idea...

79

How did it go?

Q **I did the preparation thoroughly, went in and showed it. My boss said I was being too inflexible, that I had prejudged the result of the interview and that she had some ideas for me as well. How do I recover?**

A *Yes, you have a boss who prepares carefully as well. You probably hit her with too many ideas and surprises at once. It's not easy, but having decided the route you want to take, you needed to help her to feel that actually it was all her idea. The situation you are in now means that you are going to have to take her suggestions very seriously at least for the present. Next time talk to her during the two to three weeks before your career discussion. Suggest some possibilities, leak one or two aspirations, and thank and congratulate her when she comes to a conclusion that suits you.*

Q **I wrote my job description and it went down well with my boss. It does mean that a number of people in the team need to change how they work with me. How do I tell them about that without getting up their noses?**

A *Don't. Get your boss to do it. In fact, encourage your boss to launch the new way of doing things as though it was all his idea. That way any unhappiness in the team will be aimed at him.*

Q **Appraisal, what appraisal? What do you do if the organisation has no formal appraisal system?**

A *Pretend it does. Organise regular meetings with your boss and make sure you discuss your performance and your career at them. Hey, if you keep away from the dreaded 'appraisal' word you could be the only person in the organisation using such meetings to their advantage.*

20

I'm from head office and I'm here to help

Some managers believe that taking a staff job is dropping out of the career battle, since most power lies with line management. A thinking careerist will, however, see opportunity in a stint out of the front line.

Staff work broadens the mind.

At the heart of any organisation sits the head office with its company-wide functions of personnel, marketing, finance and so forth. Taking a secondment or a job there for a limited period of time can give your career a huge leg up. How else could you get such terrific insight into the workings of your organisation? Think of what you enjoy doing and work out how you can get yourself a role that involves doing just that.

Me, I enjoyed the coaching and training side of being a line manager and gladly accepted a role in the sales training department of the computer giant I worked for in my mid-thirties. It was good for my career. I got to see just about anyone I wanted by going to ask them how we should be doing the training. Consultation with the line tends to make a staff project better, and it's great high-level exposure.

Here's an idea for you...

The inverse of this idea is also brilliant. When you are in the line, always welcome opportunities to help staff people. Meet them in their consultation phase, be the visiting manager at a training course and attend their conferences to express the field manager's view. It's excellent networking and once again offers great insights.

SELL HIGH, SELL WIDE

In fact, how's this for a career opportunity? When I was in my staff role, my company launched a new range of products. There was to be a big splash at launch date, with presentations all round the country. The organisers of the presentations looked to sales training for help in coaching the speakers and I got the job. I helped many teams with their presentations including the French team, which I could just about help with my schoolboy French (and knowing the English version off by heart helped!). So impressed were the organisers by this that they asked me to do the Belgian team as well. I settled down with the French script in front of me and asked them to begin. They started to speak – in Flemish. Because they had to use a fair number of English words I could actually follow where they were, and I suddenly realised that they had cut a bit from the script. I stopped them and asked them why and they looked at each other in wonder that a man had learnt Flemish so quickly. But I digress.

Members of the main board were to attend the biggest press presentation in London and they duly arrived for their rehearsal. At the end there was to be a question time with six directors, including the Chairman, taking questions from the floor. I got them to practice this, with me simulating the press. Now, of course, I knew all the problems as well as the benefits that the new range would bring to customers, particularly during the changeover period from the old technology to the new. I tied them in knots! I pushed them to the limit of their technical and business knowledge. At one point a director complained about my questions. The Chairman stepped in to my rescue and said, 'No, this is great. If we can survive Ken's questions the editor of *Computer Weekly* will be a pushover.' Selling high and wide or what?

For more on networking try
IDEA 26, *What goes around comes around.*

Try another idea...

'*One staff officer jumped right over another staff officer's back,*
And another staff officer jumped right over that other staff officer's back,
A third staff officer jumped right over two other staff officers' backs,
And a fourth staff officer jumped right over all the other staff officers' backs.
They were only playing leapfrog,
They were only playing leapfrog,
They were only playing leapfrog,
When one staff officer jumped right over another staff officer's back.'
'They were only playing leapfrog', traditional First World War song

Defining idea...

83

Q **I'm in sales, and bonuses are a considerable part of my salary. Are you suggesting I give this up and take a job that, even if I go up a grade or two, will not give me as much money as I earn in the field?**

A *I hope not. There is a good argument that says if you want to get salespeople into staff jobs you have to somehow recompense them for the loss of bonus with salary in lieu. Try explaining that if they don't do that, the only salespeople who will take staff jobs or secondments are the ones who are not making their numbers and therefore won't miss out on bonuses.*

Q **My experience is that when people go into staff jobs they have every intention of coming back into the field, and their managers have agreed to take them back in, say, two years. When the time comes, however, their motivation to come back at the same level is low, and the manager who made the promise to bring them back has moved on.**

A *You're right, that is my experience too. But frequently they don't want to come back because they have found another route to the top. The end of a secondment is a good time to rethink the old career and look for line opportunities in a different part of the business. In my case, for example, I decided at the end of my stint in sales training to leave that company and start up a training company with a couple of people I met during the staff job.*

Q **I think you're underestimating how quickly the water closes over your head when you leave a job and how totally the field forgets about you when you take time out.**

A *Since you understand the danger, you can work out the remedy. Keep in touch, dammit. Find a way in your new role to help them back in the field in some way. Anyhow, with a bit of luck you will have raised your level of contact so far that there will be lots of jobs out there for you and you won't need to go back anyway.*

21

Ready, aim, fire

Keeping someone in your team who plainly is not going to make it can be very bad for your career. Your business performance suffers by definition and your boss sees you vacillating on an important issue, avoiding doing the right thing because it is uncomfortable.

Try not to create a dedicated enemy. Every manager has to sack someone from time to time. In fact some senior managers regard it is a key management skill. If you have to sack someone, timing is vital; but equally important is how you do it.

Don't forget how small a world the upper reaches of any industry are. You come across people whom you served as a customer, or for whom you worked, frequently enough for you to want to ensure that you only make enemies when there is no alternative. You may also come across people who worked for you in an earlier life, which means, of course, that that you may come across people whom you fired.

Sometimes the Human Resources rules cause a hold-up. HR is, of course, quite right to protect the company's position and make sure that you do nothing that would prejudice that. But if the delay is going to cause problems, argue strongly that the company should buy its way out of it. This is often a time to spend the organisation's money lavishly.

Sacking people is not a job that most managers find pleasant. Here are the does and don'ts:

- Do prepare carefully, not only for the meeting but also for what will happen in personnel terms after it.

- Don't let the firee talk you out of it. If you've made your decision, stick to it. You will never recover with this person if you change your mind.

- Do have a stiff drink before the meeting. You need to look assertive, firm and friendly, not a nervous wreck.

- Don't relax too much. Jokes might not go down too well right now.

- Do give a generous if not lavish settlement. This sugars the pill greatly and if you go beyond the company's norms, the person you are firing will know that it is you being generous, not the rules.

- Do go through the process meticulously. It is important that it is you who gives the generous settlement not an industrial tribunal.

Defining idea...

'Never flinch – make up your own mind and do it.'
MARGARET THATCHER

IT'S A JUNGLE OUT THERE: TRY A HEADHUNTER

For another occasion to spend the company's money lavishly look at IDEA 27, *You can't overestimate real vanity.*

Try another idea...

Now's the time to consider the value of headhunters to your career. Headhunters are something else you should spend the organisation's money lavishly on – not difficult given what these guys charge. But they have an encyclopaedic knowledge of your industry and the people and opportunities in it. They have to have; and they are very brazen about contacting people and keeping up to date. Perhaps you could help the person you are firing meet with a headhunter you know. That can sugar the pill. At the same time, encourage the headhunters to make suggestions to you at any time, not just when you want people or want a job for someone else. That way you are also encouraging them to do the same in terms of job opportunities for you.

Be very careful of the current fad for 'head-shunting'. This avoids the painful process of sacking someone by getting a headhunter to place a person you are trying to get rid of with another company. In theory, you avoid the expense of severance pay, and remove any threat of being sued for wrongful dismissal. But it would seem that someone who discovers that the ploy has been visited on them can still sue for unfair dismissal, and if the receiving company believes it has been duped, it also might have a case.

'Aim high and achieve this by moving upwards between well-regarded organisations every two years.'
P.R. WILLIAMS, HR Director, Vodafone Airtouch

Defining idea...

How did it go?

Q **I finally bit the bullet and fired a guy, having put it off for about a year longer than I should. The problem is that while people knew he was not that good he was very likeable. Why has team morale gone south big time?**

A *Team leadership jargon calls this 'grieving'. It happens when a team is reeling from a sudden change in personnel and will take a period of adjustment to get back on track. The danger here is that they will go back to an earlier stage in the building of the team and start to jockey for position and to struggle again to promote their individual ideas as the only way forward. You might choose to hold an event with a senior manager addressing the team and thanking them for their good work. That can have the impact of closure and moving on to the next phase without the person you fired.*

Q **I've got to do it next week. My boss says that I should escort the person off the premises immediately. Is she right?**

A *If there is a major security threat then, yes, she's right. But remember that you may come across the person again in your career, and this can look very brutal. I'm going to wimp out here and say that it depends on the situation and the person. Thinking back to two occasions when I did it, I got the first one to go directly because I knew they would go straight to a competitor. The other person I gave whatever time he wanted to work out his notice, or not. If I hadn't done that I believe the negative impact on my team would have been huge.*

22

You've done what?

Go-getters take risks and sometimes risks go wrong. When things go wrong people can get upset and angry. Sometimes doing the right thing for your career means that you have to deal with or even provoke someone's anger.

What happens when you stir up a hornets' nest? you might just find it works out in your favour.

An old trooper of a colleague of mine, John, had a problem client Alan. Alan never accepted that John and his company were doing the best job they could and giving a good service. He did what probably the worst of customers do – he kicked a willing horse. Alan was the training manager of a huge international company. The managing director of the company didn't see the need to meet the people who were training her staff, so John couldn't get round Alan and talk sense to her. John took this quietly for a while until he felt that the success of the client as well as the success of his company was threatened by this difficult, or ugly, person.

Here's an idea for you... **Never try to reason with an angry person. Never go back with any aggression towards an angry person. Apologise. If you feel you have nothing to apologise for then at least say you are sorry that the person is upset. Try to find something to be sympathetic about; perhaps by saying that, yes, they have every right to be angry and that you would be angry in their place. Offer to meet them again later, or if you are on the phone offer to go and see them. Don't try to look for a solution to the problem until the heat is out of the scene, perhaps not even that day.**

PLANNING THE STRATEGY

Alan was a cold, clinical bully. He got his own way without raising his voice or losing his temper in any way. He was a frustrating man. 'Right,' thought John, 'what is the objective here?' He decided he had to get to the MD, impress her with some new ideas and start a new way of taking training forward with much less interference from Alan. A bold course was called for: he would deliberately make Alan angry. He reasoned that an angry Alan would get on the phone to Brian, John's boss, and complain very vociferously. Brian would write to Alan's MD suggesting that they had to meet to bring the relationship back into line. They would play it by ear from there.

CARRYING IT THROUGH

During their next telephone call John started to get angry with Alan; instead of holding back as usual he let rip and called Alan a lot of names including one of the few words rarely printed in full. He banged the phone down and strolled into Brian's office.

'I've just called Alan a c***.' 'You've done what?' gasped Brian, 'I've just called Alan a c***' repeated John. 'But you shouldn't have done that.' 'I know I shouldn't have done it, but I have. So let's work out what we do about it.' "But… but… but… you shouldn't have done that.' 'Yes, Brian I know that; so what do you suggest we do?' At that moment Brian's phone rang and the first part of the strategy had worked. On the line was an absolutely furious Alan.

Do you want to know the end of the John story? The strategy worked inasmuch as Brian got into see the MD and a new relationship was formed. John, however, was not part of this new arrangement. Alan refused point blank to deal with him. Over a drink one night John confided to me that being pulled off the account was his plan B.

FINALLY

Ambitious people do not duck issues because they fear a person's anger; rather they learn to deal with it.

For more information on handling 'ugly' managers look at IDEA 36, *What do you recommend?*

Try another idea…

'Anyone can become angry. That is easy. But to be angry with the right person, to the right degree, at the right time, for the right purpose and in the right way – that is not easy.'
ARISTOTLE

Defining idea…

Q **I remembered this idea this morning when I went in to the marketing department and found that my lot had completely ruined an expensive carpet by not covering it up while they repainted the false ceiling. I apologised whole-heartedly, and eventually a very angry manager calmed down. 'Right,' I said 'Let's work out what we need to do to get this carpet as back to normal as we possibly can.' Then, guess what? She kicked off again, bringing up an array of incidents that I remembered from some time back when there had been other glitches in the maintenance service?**

A *Ah yes, sorry, I should have mentioned that. When people get angry and start to complain they rarely keep to a single point. They will rake up old faults, sometimes very old ones. You have to make sure they have got it all off their chest before reason gets a chance. Ask questions like, 'I think we should take this opportunity to look at the performance of the whole maintenance service we provide. Are there any other places where you feel we have fallen down?'*

Q **There's one other thing. When she was going on about the lack of responsiveness from the cleaners to her requests for a change in the time they did her part of the building, I reminded her that I wasn't actually in charge at that time. That didn't go down at all well. I shouldn't have done that, should I?**

A *No. Look at IDEA 34, I'm alright, it's the others.*

23

Draw your own map

In order to get to the top you need to be seen as a strategic thinker. To get that reputation you need to do some. Strategic thinking, that is. Here's a short cut to a creating a team strategy.

The aim of this idea is simple. You are going to present a strategy for your team that is going to knock your boss's socks off and make him insist that all your colleagues copy you.

And that's the second benefit – while you're producing a first-class performance, everyone else is tying themselves in knots trying to write a strategic plan. Only you know the short cut.

The first skill involved in creating a strategy is the ability to balance short-term thinking with long-term planning. Put some long-term thinking time into your schedule. You don't have much time; you needed a strategy yesterday. And, who knows, you may need a new one tomorrow.

Once they've decided to create a strategy, most managers think they need a consultant to help them to write it. Other people think they need a facilitator to

Here's an idea for you...

It is a really good idea to check this analysis with a few people including, of course, your key customers. Don't be frightened to show them your analysis. If there are bits they don't like or don't agree with, it's better that you know now.

help the team with the process. From vast, and occasionally bitter, experience I believe it is better if you can to do it on your own. Facilitators have to be perceived to add value to the planning process, so they invent complicated procedures and forms. Actually all you need is some flipcharts, pens and one crucial technique.

Right, you've got your team in the planning room and agreed to do at least half a day on the plan, and another half day in a week's time. Write first on the flipchart your vision for the future. You should have prepared this earlier and checked it over with the key people in your team before the session. This saves hours, and if later it turns out to be not quite right you can change it during the time you are implementing the strategy.

THE PLANNING TECHNIQUES

Use SWOT analysis as the analytical part of the process. Ask the team: in terms of achieving our vision, what are our strengths, weaknesses, opportunities and threats. Don't get hung up on words. Get the ideas down. Remember that you are all going to be living with this plan forever. But it will evolve constantly. you don't have to get it spot on at your first meeting.

And now follows the bit where a lot of teams go wrong. You've got to get from analysis strategic goals and action plan. Give each weakness, opportunity and threat an identifying number. (Ignore the strengths for now.) Write down the following topics: people, skills, facilities, customers and suppliers. Allocate each weakness, opportunity and threat to one of those topics. If some will not fit, choose another key word – it's unusual to need more than six or seven. Now allocate each topic to one or two team members. Send them away to work out the goals the team should set in that area and the actions necessary to achieve this. Tell them that the strengths might give some clues for the action plan. At a second meeting the following week discuss and agree the goals and actions, allocate the actions to a team member – and you have a strategic plan!

You really need to know what your organisation's strategy is before you embark on creating your own. IDEA 18, *Find out what you're supposed to be doing*, will help with this.

Try another idea...

Throughout the process be prepared to question and challenge accepted norms. The really upwardly mobile careerist will fight tooth and nail before acknowledging that something the company is doing wrong cannot be changed. But watch the politics. It's a tough call, but you have to judge whether your boss's entrenched views can now be challenged by you and your team. In my experience, though, the safety-first acquiescence path is so much easier to contemplate that most people err on that side rather than taking the risk of becoming known as a doubter or, worse, a troublemaker. Courage, *mon brave*, nobody said life was easy.

Prepare to shine. You have a strategy and it is written down. Tell people about it, partly because you are trying to build your career and partly because you want to influence others towards your way of thinking. Make presentations. Sell your methodology to others so that you become the source of the company-wide strategic planning system. And then sit back and watch your colleagues suffer.

'Strategies are intellectually simple; their execution is not.'
LARRY BOSSIDY, industrialist

Defining idea...

How did it go?

Q **OK, I'm doing this and two members of the team don't agree with an important part of the plan where they needed to change what they do. Any thoughts on why this should be?**

A *I wonder. Perhaps they do not feel they have the skills to go into the new areas. What about talking them through training or coaching or whatever will help them feel more confident in the new role? Don't forget though that some people can't change. It could be curtains for them in your team if they can't fit in with the strategy.*

Q **I thought this was brilliant to begin with. We did it more or less as you suggested although it took more time than you said. It's a good plan, pushing to change and make improvements in a number of areas. How do we make all these changes and at the same time hit our operational targets? They already constitute a full time job.**

A *Welcome to the world of strategic thinking. Prioritise the goals and actions. Choose a small number that will make it easier to hit the operational targets with less effort. Put the others on hold. Look for one that gives a real short-term result, because it's good for team morale and another opportunity to show off.*

24

Keep up the good work

Some of your best career promoters are the members of your team. If they speak with pride of their department and warmly about you senior managers will notice. Replace someone who is running a happy team with great care. You've got to maintain performance and get them on your side.

You can't be a clone of your predecessor. Would you rather take over a team with a positive mental attitude or a bunch of demoralised grumblers? The former could be waiting for you to fail to live up to your glorious predecessor.

This happened to me when I took over a team from Martin, who had got himself a neat promotion after producing very good results and this very happy team.

Martin was a very quick thinker, he was also tactically bold and 100 per cent sure of himself – the perfect mixture for an autocratic manager. The team came to him for everything; no one else took decisions, not even small ones. I knew that I couldn't work like that. It wasn't my style, I didn't think it developed the individuals in the team – besides it looked like bloody hard work and by nature I'm a bit of a skiver.

Here's an idea for you...

When you take over a new job, watch out for the people who stay completely loyal to your predecessor and take every opportunity to rubbish you. They can have a huge impact on the team, particularly the junior and younger members, and they are almost certainly pouring poison into your boss's ear as well. This is a time to be ruthless. Get shot of them now. Don't wait for the rotten apple to spread the disease.

Try another idea...

Have a look at IDEA 4, *Don't come to me with your problems*.

Defining idea...

'No man will make a great leader who wants to do it all himself, or to get all the credit for doing it.'
ANDREW CARNEGIE, industrialist

I thought about it long and hard and discussed the situation with one of my mentors; then I came up with a plan. In the first week I arranged to meet every member of the team individually for a 45-minute slot. During the quiet 15 minutes between appointments I read a newspaper and drank coffee. In that time, of course, the door opened several times and people asked me what to do in particular situations. I developed a catchphrase response, 'I don't know mate, I'm new here.' Eventually they got the idea and I developed a new culture where people came to me with solutions not problems.

Luckily when I took over from Martin I was very careful to keep my boss up to speed. My new team really thrashed around. They looked and felt rudderless. Since I wasn't telling them what to do, they would go to my boss when I wasn't in. She handled it quite well but did give advice in some cases where I would have preferred her not to. She was concerned that what I was doing would impact performance, at least in the short term. Now, funnily enough, it didn't. Not sure why, although it is probably connected to the fact that the best people in the team quickly started to just get on with it and then they started to enjoy it, and the change had at least started.

Q **I've taken over a team of managers from one of the most respected, and I would say loved, members of the organisation. I can't do what you did because she ran a very consultative style anyway. The team is devastated. Can you work out how to handle it, because I'm struggling?**

How did it go?

A *Blimey, are you sure this was a smart career move? At the moment I can only think of avoiding the threats. The biggest threat here is a so-called 'Government in exile'. This happens when the person you took over from, particularly if you are the Chief Executive, holds regular government-in-exile board meetings. They gather all their best mates together for a social event and probably, in the nicest possible way, bitch about you like mad. Speak to your predecessor about it. Flatter her nauseatingly, really lay it on thick and ask her directly to keep her contacts with the team minimal. In fact, I think that is how I would deal with this situation. Ask her for advice; she knows the people well and will be able to help. I would also be inclined to bring at least one person you know into the team, and get rid of at least one of the original team. Then everyone knows that change is happening and that life will never be exactly the same again.*

Q **I am in the situation you describe. I'm all right with most of the team, but one of them won't change how they work. We agree how he is going to handle something and then I find that he has done something completely different. He always has brilliant reasons. It's starting to make me angry. Should I fire him?**

A   Not if he is good at his job and if the team like and respect him – or at least not yet. I am assuming that you are in quite a senior position. What about bringing in a deputy who is an old pal of yours? He can then supervise activities more closely and perhaps put in some business process that forces the man to change. Make sure the old pal is good with people, though. He has to get the rest of the team behind him.

25

Don't talk so much

It is frightening how little listening goes on. Because of this, your boss's team meetings offer an excellent opportunity for appearing authoritative and getting your own way.

We all do it, we just don't listen.

I did a small piece of research on key management skills. While not statistically valid, the response of some thirty senior business people showed a huge majority put listening at the top of their list of necessary skills. One of them called it 'active listening'.

Here is the art of listening going wrong for an architect. He had the job of advising a couple on how they should use the space and carry out the refurbishment of an old, run-down property they had just bought. Unfortunately there was a hiatus between the architect's survey and his first meeting with the new owners. He used the time to speculate on what they might want to do with the house. What did it lack, in his view, and what would they have to do to put that lack right?

The owners arrived for the first meeting with a list of their requirements for the property. Despite this, the architect went ahead and presented the ideas that he had already sketched. After all, that's human nature. We all want to show our original ideas off since they feel so right to us. The architect was in fact interrupting the

Here's an idea for you...

At your boss's next team meeting don't leap in with your views. Listen until everyone has spoken, assimilate what has been said and eventually summarise the substance. By that time you will know where your interests lie and be able to steer the meeting towards them.

Defining idea...

'If you know the enemy and know yourself, you need not fear the result of a hundred battles. If you know yourself but not the enemy, for every victory gained you will also suffer a defeat. If you know neither the enemy nor yourself, you will succumb in every battle.'

SUN TZU, *The Art of War*

customer to make a point. When the customer eventually tabled the list, it was very different from the first thoughts of their adviser. They now had a situation of the customer not wanting to make the adviser feel bad, and the adviser feeling the need to defend his work. Despite all that went after, the relationship never got over this appalling start. Please don't ignore this story because you think that you would never do that. Keep quiet at your next meeting and just watch people, even senior people, not listening at all.

Like all skills you get better at listening if you practice it. Here's an exercise I got from Penny Ferguson. Get yourself and a colleague, or if that's difficult a member of your family, to sit down in comfortable chairs facing each other. Now explain that you are going to listen to them for three minutes without any interruption. Then give them the topic. Ask them to talk for three minutes about things that they appreciate about themselves. Now settle down to do some active listening. Keep your eyes steady on them, although theirs will probably wander as they think about the question. For many people this is quite difficult. Normally we would be in there talking, advising and correcting, but that's not the point.

Here's another statistically invalid finding from my experience. Women in business are instinctively better at this than men. So women, be careful that your listening does not look as though you have no ideas. And men, for pity's sake don't talk so much!

You may be interested in **IDEA 47, Be successful whatever your gender.**

Try another idea...

'The first component we have to put in place to help our people think very well is for them to know that they are listened to, for them to know that they have somebody's undivided attention. And by undivided attention I mean you focus on them 100 per cent of the time. Your eyes are on them, sending this message, "I am fascinated by what you are thinking about and saying."'
PENNY FERGUSON, personal leadership guru

Defining idea...

How did it go?

Q **I'm in hot competition with another upwardly mobile person on my boss's team. We tend to disagree on principle and I think my boss is starting not to like it. How can I agree with my rival without looking as though his ideas are providing leadership?**

A *This is tricky to organise but devastating in its effect. Table an issue where you know this person and your boss have different views. When your man is expounding on this issue encourage him like mad by smiling and nodding agreement. People in that situation tend to deliver the whole speech to the nodder. He might just miss any warning signals coming from your boss and dig himself a hole.*

Q **Right, I tried listening. I know I tend to dominate my monthly team meetings. At the last one I made sure that I listened to what people were saying much more than I usually do. Everybody talked more than they usually do, but the meeting dragged on and they found it difficult to come to a conclusion for each agenda item.**

A *Brilliant! You are getting the hang of it. Now learn better chairing skills so that you help the team to make solid progress in a reasonable time. Encourage yourself by thinking about all the things you heard and learnt at that meeting that you would not have normally known anything about.*

26

What goes around comes around

Most people start networking when they are unhappy in their job or have been made redundant. Too late. Put your network of contacts to work on your career at all times. You never know when someone you used to know comes around again.

Bear in mind the endgame, now.

The endgame of a brilliant career includes some non-executive directorships. It's a good life. You are paid a modest sum of money a year for preparing for and attending a board meeting every month. If asked, you can always take on a one-off project on behalf of the board, to keep your hand in. And if it gets a little niffy or unpleasant, like the grandchildren you simply hand the problem back to the people who own it and just walk away. But to get these directorships you need to push.

There are many things I like about politicians but one thing above all. They wear their ambition on their sleeves. Seldom do they try to hide the fact that they are playing to win, and winning means getting more and more power. They expect us to think that. They seem to relish the battle and to pursue their careers even though they must be aware that almost all of them, when they eventually succumb to the people's will, are going to be denigrated and probably despised by their

Here's an idea for you... **Make a regular plan for staying in contact with a wide range of people in your address book. I don't mean a circular letter at Christmas; just a personal note asking how they are doing. This keeps your name alive, triggers thoughts and will give rise to all sorts of opportunities.**

conquerors. Yet such is their vanity or their self-belief – or both – that they plunge into the fray. It is easy to use words like battle and war in this context, and when you come down to it, in the business environment as well. It's either you or someone else. One gets the glory and the other stays in a job that firstly bores them, secondly irritates them and finally embitters them.

So, if you're in business you may as well join the mêlée and cut loose your ambition. You need to stand out in the crowd and get yourself noticed. If you want to join the board, people must see you as utterly unflappable and competent. They must notice that you are normally right and always confident. You will make them feel their own inadequacies. But how do you close the business and get the job? Well, you start now by keeping in contact with people you have worked with or for, with old customers and with suppliers. Henry Lewis, a former CEO of Marks & Spencer, was offered non-execs by many of his suppliers. One of them was so keen that it kept back a sizable chunk of shares so that it could offer them to Harry when he retired in exchange for his coming on to its board.

KEEP A LIFETIME ADDRESS BOOK

Look at it this way. Some companies place such value on their database of knowledge of their customers and prospective customers that they quantify it and put it on the balance sheet as an intangible asset. Companies have changed hands because one bought another for its market information, and mergers have taken place where the only real synergy was complementary customer lists. Your version of this is your address book. Never take anyone off it. You never know when they might come in useful. Organise it in sections so that you have a reminder of where and why you met each contact.

A good source of opportunity in the non-exec area is the older members of the senior management team. Have a look at IDEA 32, *Help the aged.*

Try another idea...

A man who was on a training course that my colleague John ran some fifteen years ago rang him up recently. Since the man was in the delegate section of his address book John was able to demonstrate his remarkable memory. He also had recorded the opinions of himself and the other managers running the course on how good they thought this guy was at the time. All of this proved invaluable: now a senior manager, this man is currently one of John's prospective clients.

I have never met anyone who has kept a long-term address book say that it has been a waste of time. I have heard many regret that they didn't. I'm one of them, dammit.

'The people who get on in this world are the people who get up and look for the circumstances they want, and, if they can't find them, make them.'
GEORGE BERNARD SHAW

Defining idea...

How did
it go?

Q **I've been pretty systematic in communicating with my network, but don't you find that making contact often goes the opposite way? When I contact old colleagues, for instance, the ones who come back to me are almost always the ones who are looking for help in their careers. One of them continues to pester me for a job a year after my note to him. Surely I can take him off the list?**

A *I wouldn't if I were you. In the chaos of the business world I have stopped being amazed at some of the people who make it big. One of the people on my graduate trainee intake was seen as pretty useless by the rest of us. He is now a knight and advises government on various issues. I should have kept in contact.*

Q **Another thing. I sent one of your little notes to a person I used to sell to some years ago. They were very friendly in return and suggested lunch. It was a fairly gruesome affair. I knew very quickly that there was no way our careers were going to connect again, and it was just a big (and not inexpensive) bore.**

A *Do a bit more qualifying before you agree to the sort of time involved in lunch, and filter out those you think can't help. But sometimes, yes, you have to swim through some treacle.*

27

Vain, who *moi?*

Choosing how to interact with senior managers is key to career development. Here are some thoughts about deference, flattery and managing vanity, all vital ingredients of your relationship with the top folk.

Look after your seniors. Senior managers are all different. When you're about to meet one for the first time make sure you've prepared properly by talking to people in the know.

But you can make some assumptions and one of these is that they will be vain. All human beings are to some extent vain. Top managers are somewhat larger-than-life human beings; therefore top managers tend to have as high a level of vanity as any normal human being, and higher than most.

Tom, a friend of mine, was a manager in the Edinburgh office of a US company. He was about to get a historic visit from the CEO. Tom knew that his counterpart in the Manchester office, Mike, was to have his visit a few days earlier. The plan in each case was that the CEO would fly up from London and spend two days visiting the offices and meeting customers. There would be a customer dinner on the evening of the first day. Tom asked Mike about his preparations. 'Well,' said Mike, 'It's

Here's an idea for you...

Think through your next exposure to a senior manager whom you wish to impress. How can you play to their vanity? How will you feed their pride without appearing nauseating?

difficult. You know that we are being told to save on expenses at the moment, tightening our belts and so forth, so I thought that we should show that we take that seriously and keep the whole visit fairly low key.' 'Really,' said Tom. 'Yes,' continued Mike, 'I thought we would pick him up in a normal first-line manager's company car, that would show thrift, and put him up in the same hotel we use for the graduate trainees when they join. It's pleasant but obviously not overly expensive.' He continued to describe this hair-shirt treatment. At the end of the conversation Tom called in his PA and said 'We are going to give the man a welcome to Edinburgh that makes the plans for the Queen coming up to Holyrood Palace look stingy.'

And so they did. After his visit to Manchester the CEO was not entirely looking forward to the next one. He arrived at the airport to be met by a PA with a clipboard, and was led straight past the luggage carousel to a waiting limo. The PA explained that someone else was picking up his bags.

Tom had carefully chosen where the CEO was to stay, the sort of classy Georgian Hotel that even a well-travelled executive finds unusual. A butler unpacked them and put his things away. Tom had booked a suite so that the CEO could entertain the top customers in private to drinks before they descended to join the hoi polloi for dinner. And so it went on.

Giving and receiving appreciation, however, is an important element of motivating people including you. See IDEA 39, *Two, four, six, eight.*

Try another idea...

Subsequently Tom got feedback that the CEO had loved the visit to Edinburgh. In fact he got a warm thank-you note, while Mike just got a note, and another one from his boss saying 'Don't do that again.'

Oh, Vanity of vanities!
How wayward the decrees of fate are;
How very weak the wise are,
How very small the great are!
WILLIAM MAKEPEACE THACKERAY

Defining idea...

How did it go?

Q **I supply a printing service to publishers. I am engaged in trying to win the next six in a long-running series of books. I engineered an opportunity to see the head of the division via one of the people who work for her, my key contact in the organisation. I had heard that this divisional head had actually come up with the idea for the whole series in the first place. I was fulsome in my praise for the books, how they met a need and what a good idea the series was. She, as you suggested, lapped it up big time. Trouble is that when I came out my key contact was spitting mad. She claimed that actually the idea for the series was hers. Could I have done the same thing without upsetting her?**

A *Yes, your preparation has gone wrong here. You should have known that the provenance of the idea was in dispute. If you had discussed it with your contact you could have had great fun with how you awarded the praise, amused your normal contact enormously; but still played to the vanity of the division head.*

Q **I've just seen a manager kowtowing nauseatingly to a senior guy; but the guy seemed to enjoy it. In the end the junior manager was in my view conning the senior. Is there a corollary to this idea that says you should do your best to avoid vanity yourself?**

A *Yes, I think you're right. It's a bit like Kingsley Amis saying that he was glad that finally old age had made his libido disappear because at last he was not being led by an idiot.*

28

Everybody lives by selling something

There is no cynical get-out here. You can take all the short cuts in the world but in the end your career depends on your customers doing business with you and expressing their delight with your performance. Keep them at the front of your and your team's thinking.

Keep up to date with what the customer needs.

'Through here pass the most important people in the world – our customers.' This notice is above the door of one of the worst garage workshops through which it has been my dubious pleasure to pass. The thought is right. Everyone has customers on whom they depend for their livelihood. You get to the top echelons of management if you actually deliver on that statement and treat the customer as king. Make them drive every stage of your plan. Try to think ahead of what they will require in the future. There are two kinds of manager in this respect: those who are always trying to catch up because they become aware of changes in their customer's needs after the event, and those who make changes in anticipation of this. When you get yourself ahead of the game, it will be difficult for anything to stop your success. But you've got to deliver it as well as promise it. I'd love to change that sign in the dead of the night to, 'Through here pass the most incompetent people in the world – our managers.'

Your seniors will pay more attention to a customer who praises you than to anyone else. So make it happen. When something has gone well, and assuming you have a close relationship with your customer, get them to write a thank-you note to you, copied to the most senior person they know in your organisation, preferably at least your boss's boss. Time this to coincide with another key event, your appraisal maybe, or your big request for more resources. But don't overdo it or your boss will know that it is you setting it up.

GET EVERYONE TO TALK TO THEM

Keep your organisation in touch with reality, by making sure that no one can completely evade customer contact. You can do this individually by insisting your product developer, for example, attends customer progress meetings, or *en masse* by inviting the customer to come and speak at the annual get together. Invite your boss as well. If getting everyone to meet the customer is a new idea, you could be doing your career no harm at all if you introduce this. Engineers, for example, sometimes completely transform the way they think about their work once they have got a real insight into what the customers are trying to do, and how they look at their offerings.

The finance department may seem an unlikely contender for customer contact. But suppose that you ran the financial control department for an organisation based in several locations, none of which is in your building. You wouldn't consider trying to operate without going to see the various sites. You need to get a feel for what they have to deal with. Indeed, if you don't get some of your own people out there as

Defining idea...

'The future belongs to those who prepare for it today.'
MALCOLM X

well, you could well be failing to tap into an important source of insights. If your people visit the sites from time to time, they'll probably see how they can make simple changes. You, the manager, may have missed it because of your lack of intimate knowledge of the details.

In the same way it is vital for your finance people, for example, to get direct knowledge of your customers. Get them face to face with customers, and get them amenable to any changes that the customer requests. That way your customers will realise how professional whole team serving them is, and your career will soar on the wings of customer satisfaction.

See if **IDEA 30, *Learn to love your sales force*, gives some clues for dealing with this.**

Try another idea...

'The best way to predict the future is to create it.'
PETER DRUCKER, management thinker

Defining idea...

How did
it go?

Q **I tried getting some of my software development team leaders to attend a meeting with the customer where the customer made a presentation about her needs and we spoke of our plans. The formal part went quite well; it was chatting over coffee afterwards that things went a bit awry. One of my people talked about a future development we are planning. The customer loved it and wants it now. It's given us a problem and my boss didn't like it. How do you guard against that?**

A *Better briefing, I'm afraid. Make sure they understand the limitations on customer contact. In general I find that engineers will stick more closely to a brief than other functions. But plan the meetings carefully.*

Q **I run a finance team. They hate our salespeople whom they regard as overpaid charlatans. If I try to make them think about their jobs as having a selling angle don't I run the risk of huge resistance?**

A *Possibly. Use the words 'customer satisfaction' rather than selling to begin with and then move towards understanding the customer better – 'marketing.' Then take the stabilisers off and confess that it's actually 'selling'. Now, I know I said expose everyone to the customer, but don't go mad. If you really do have someone who thinks selling is dishonest, who knows what they might say to the customer. You might be better keeping them in the backroom.*

29

Changing horses mid-career

If you make a move to a new company your fellow managers there have an advantage over you. They know the ropes and how to shine in the existing environment. It is therefore a very good idea to do something early on to question that environment and change it in a high-profile way.

When you are changing employer think long and hard about why they hired you.

If you are joining at a fairly high level it is likely that the people who hired you saw you as an agent of change, for a part of their business or culture which is underperforming – new blood, new brooms and all that. If this is the case, you can afford to take a few risks in the early days.

MAKE A SPLASH, WHY DON'T YOU?

Here's a brilliant example of making a great splash early on in a new outfit. A manager I know moved from one telecommunications company to another much larger and longer established one. He knew, from his competitive knowledge and from things said at the interview, that senior management were implementing a huge programme of change aimed at knocking the old-fashioned corners off those managers who had served with the organisation since the year dot.

Here's an idea for you...

Even if you are staying put in your organisation have a long, hard think about change. What in your company really needs to be changed? Think deeply and don't be held back by things that seem to be cast in stone – nothing is. Right, if the change is within your authority, just do it. If it's not in your authority, but it wouldn't be a suicidal risk, just do it anyway. If it's too much of a risk to take on yourself, go to the person who could do it and persuade them to let you do it. Try not to give them the whole idea or they might pinch it.

Many of these people were accustomed to a hierarchical, rather deferential culture where seniority counted highly. They were also struggling with the idea that the customer was king. On his very first day the new boy took action using the car park as his vehicle, if you'll pardon the pun. He removed every car parking space allocated on the basis of management seniority, and reallocated the best spaces to customers only. As he was doing this he realised that some areas were not only dark but also outside the range of the security cameras. So he allocated the next best spaces nearest to the entrance to those women who sometimes or regularly worked late.

At a stroke he got the support of those of his people who felt held back by the old guard, and of the more ambitious women willing to work long hours. His action also became high profile without his having to tell a soul – the old guard did it for him: they were fuming. They sent angry e-mails to the HR department and senior managers in all parts of the organisation complaining about this loss of their hard-earned privilege. They themselves gave him the oxygen of publicity. By the end of his very first day he had a very high profile. He had sorted the resisters to change from the enthusiasts for it, and impressed on senior management his grasp of what they were looking for in terms of cultural change. Senior management congratulated themselves, modestly of course, for hiring the right person for the job.

IDEA 41, *The rule of 20 per cent*, gives some guidance on getting change to stick in an organisation.

Try another idea...

'*Most ideas on management have been around for a very long time, and the skill of the manager consists in knowing them all and, rather as he might choose the appropriate golf club for a specific situation, choosing the particular ideas which are most appropriate for the position and time in which he finds himself.'*
SIR JOHN HARVEY-JONES, former ICI chief

Defining idea...

How did it go?

Q   **I loved this idea and decided to have a go at a matter that has annoyed for many years – implementing IT. We have always felt forced to buy our IT services from the outsource company who took over our IT department some time ago. One of my managers has been saying that in one area particularly we could get a better service, and cheaper, if we did it ourselves. I told him to go ahead in a note that I copied to IT. Bloody hell, two days later I have the CEO's office on the line telling me not to do it. Can you imagine how I feel about the idea now?**

A   *Still completely positive, if you ask me. This is brilliant. You are now in a position to go direct to the CEO to explain your idea. Get your bloke to write up the business case and send it to the CEO as your reply to their note. Sock it to them pal, there are few sweeter things in business life than getting the boffins in the IT department on the run. What a result! By the way, copying the original note to IT was asking for permission which, I thought we had agreed, is never as easy as asking for forgiveness. But in this case it has worked out just fine.*

Q   **Why is car parking always such a sensitive issue?**

A   *I'm not sure – but one hoary old MD advised me never to have enough car parking spaces because it gives everyone a focus for complaint. If you solve that one they might notice that they're also badly paid and working in other awful conditions.*

30

Count your fingers

Yep, this one is about the sales force. You have to learn to love them, because using a key customer as their torpedo, they can hole anyone's career below the water-line. Here's a way of understanding them that gives you a fighting chance of dealing with them effectively.

What's the problem?

Many organisations fear their salespeople. They seem to be young for the money they can make and often only come to the attention of the rest of the company if something has gone wrong (when, for example, the business is spending time and money trying to deliver a salesperson's promises). Nowadays, it is vital to remove this fear and replace it with a wary respect for the front-line job. That way your career and the sellers will all march in the same direction.

So, how do you set about getting your team to love your salespeople?

KNOW THE ANIMAL YOU'RE TRYING TO WORK WITH

Make sure, in the first place, that everyone understands that the selling job is divided into 'hunting' or 'farming'. Hunting is about bringing in new customers, farming about increasing the amount of business you do with your existing customers. The skills are different and a major recruitment consideration is how much of each activity the job involves. If you deal with your salespeople in the

Here's an idea for you...

If the sales force is on a straight commission on sales then they won't be fully motivated to get orders at list price. Make sure that any drop in profits caused by their discounting is reflected in their wallets. A 10 per cent discount on the sales price has little impact on the salesperson's income but may have reduced bottom-line profit by more than 33 per cent. If it's easy to administer, a lot of managers use the gross profit of a deal as the basis for sales bonuses, and this works quite well. The other possibility is to discount the sales bonus pro rata to the sales discount, so 90 per cent of list price will yield, say, only 50 per cent of the full sales bonus.

wrong mode you'll have problems. Particularly if you treat a hunter as though she's a farmer.

For hunters the main requirements are persistence and the ability to take knocks. Their job involves trying to get interviews with strangers who may not only be unaware of their need but antagonistic to an unsolicited approach.

Hunters generally work quickly, have short attention spans and feel very dissatisfied if complications of product or decision-making processes prevent them closing a sale. They are opportunists and in most cases need watching to make sure that they don't promise results your product can't deliver.

Some would say that it is the hunters who give salespeople a bad name. There is some truth in that, but they are also the people who make innovation possible and *en masse* bear a lot of responsibility for driving the dollar round in a growth economy.

Here's a hunter talking, 'You actually have to start by getting yourself invited into the buyer's office. Then you must convince a probable sceptic that what you are offering has benefits over continuing with the people they are using at present.

If sales people still make your toes curl, see if IDEA 30, *Two, four, six, eight*, might help

Try another idea...

'Then you have to find a project, bid for it and win it. The great feeling is that you made it happen; if you had not made the first move, that company would have remained loyal to its existing suppliers.'

Many people find the prospect of hunting horrendous; but organisations are recognising more and more their dependence on such people.

Farmers develop skills in long-term relationship building and deep knowledge of a customer's business. The benefits to management of professional farmers are predictable orders, competitive intelligence, awareness of market changes and much more.

'He's a man way out there in the blue, riding on a smile and a shoeshine. And when they start not smiling back – that's an earthquake...A salesman is got to dream. It comes with the territory.'
ARTHUR MILLER, *Death of a Salesman*

Defining idea...

FINALLY

Maybe it's impossible to get everyone to love the sales force; but if you can't do that at least make sure they are talking to the right animal. Talk fast, short and assertively to the hunter, analytically with the farmer.

Q **This is quite clever.**   *A* *Thank you.*

Q **Well not that clever, pal.**   *A* *Whatever.*

Q **You've explained what I was doing wrong with a salesperson that you would define as a hunter. I have been trying to explain technically and analytically the specification that he needs to put into a proposal he is working on. I sit him down and I show him the facts. He glazes over, his eyes wander; he even gets his phone out and checks for messages when I am in mid-flow. He then goes off and continues to promise something that we won't be able to deliver. I've kept calm but only just. How can I make him see sense?**

A *I'm afraid you probably can't. Go up his management line until you come to an experienced sales manager who is also a farmer. They will sort him out. He'll do it with short simple sentences like 'If you don't change the proposal you're fired.' Almost always works.*

Q **In my team I've got an excellent technical person who will have nothing to do with the salespeople. He thinks they are liars and corrupt because of the number of times he has had to bale out customers from situations where our rep had over-inflated their expectations.**

A *Assuming that the systems are in place to check the feasibility of what the salesperson is allowed to propose, this man has a problem. Ask the sales director to speak to him and explain what competitive pressures the salespeople are working in.*

31

Make them agree fast

What do you want from your brilliant career? It's probably a mix of money, status, fun and finally power or influence. Let's look at the last of these, and find a way you can get agreement quickly to any proposal, big or small. This method is quick to prepare and must be reuseable.

Show them how to make the decision.

Most managers are familiar with showing the benefits of a proposal to an audience. 'What's in it for them?' 'What does it actually do for the bottom line?' Well, we've had this dinged into us enough times during various training courses. And it's true. You are more likely to be convincing if you spell out the benefits of your proposition from the recipient's point of view rather than take the risk of allowing them to do it, or not do it, for themselves.

How about showing people 'how' to make the decision? This takes user-friendly propositions to the next level by adding another topic. So far we are all convinced that you present a proposal like this:

- Problem or opportunity
- Your proposed solution
- Benefits to the audience of the proposed solution

Here's an idea for you... **Take an idea you are trying to persuade your boss or your team to accept. Write down the features of your solution and then turn them into a basis of decision. Some will be dead easy because they truly have merit when seen from the audience's point of view. Some will be difficult, probably don't pass the 'so what's in it for me test' and should be discarded.**

I want to add another element between the presentation of the problem and your solution – let's call it the *basis of decision*. Here are a few of examples of the practical bases of decision suggested by a seller of insurance policies to opticians:

- The package should include all principal business needs in one policy.

- The administrators of the scheme must have a lot of experience in your type of business.

- The insurance cover must be tailored to your business without losing its cost competitiveness.

- The underwriters must be first-rank UK-based companies.

Now, the salesperson could have promoted exactly the same ideas by banging on about the product she's selling. 'My product includes all the principal business needs in one policy. The administrators of my scheme have a lot of experience in your type of business.' And so on. There are two reasons why using the basis of decision approach gets better results faster in terms of persuading people that you have the right solution. The first is that it sees things from their point of view. (You often, for example, introduce the basis of decision with words like 'I understand you are looking for a solution that...' or 'Seen from your point of view you need a solution that....')

The second benefit is that you can ask if the audience agrees with the basis of decision. If you've simply dumped on them a list of product features you can't say 'Isn't that right?' because they will just say that they don't know. If they give you a positive response to your proposed basis of decision you've more or less cracked it. Just tell them that's what your solution does.

The related topic of finally putting the boot in to a committee is discussed in IDEA 35, *The multi-headed decision maker.*

Try another idea...

IT DOESN'T ALWAYS WORK

I was selling a computer to an educational establishment. They had very little money and I showed them how, if they bought a second-hand machine, they could have much more power and functionality. I took my boss's boss in to a meeting where I was hoping to close the business. I went through the basis of decision. I asked them if they agreed that I'd got it right and they did, whole-heartedly. 'Well,' said my boss's boss, 'that more or less describes our solution, so are you going to buy from us?' There was a short pause before the chairman said that there was one more thing – they didn't want to buy anything second-hand. Mmm, I'd missed that.

FINALLY

Like many effective techniques, using the basis of decision to get your own way is very simple. It's common sense, but it's not common practice. So it's good for your career and it gets result fast!

'A monologue is not a decision.'
CLEMENT ATTLEE to Winston Churchill who had complained that a matter had been raised several times in cabinet

Defining idea...

How did it go?

Q **I tried this when I was attempting to persuade a workers' committee to accept a change in their terms of employment. When I asked if they agreed that that was how they should see the decision, they said 'no' to just about everything. I just went on with the proposed solution but they never became entirely gruntled during the whole meeting. Assuming your stupid idea does work, what should I have done?**

A *Well, I think the 'stupid' idea worked 'brilliantly'. The fact is you misread their reaction to the discussion because you didn't understand how they would look at it. You should have abandoned the rest of the proposal, sat down with them and asked them what criteria were important to them in coming to a decision. Frankly, it was rather 'stupid' not to have done this before, at least with some of the key people on the committee.*

Q **I did this basis of decision thing with the advertising director when trying to get some more money out of her. I asked her if she agreed and she said yes, but that she wanted to add another criterion. This rather threw me, as the one she chose didn't really favour my proposal. I stuttered and stammered to try to fit the new criterion in. Isn't this going to happen quite often?**

A *Possibly, but if she had not come up with the new criterion then it would have emerged as an objection later on. What you do is this. Take a careful note of the new criterion and make sure you have understood exactly what she is looking for. Then go back to your proposal. You have between then and the end of the meeting to think out how to deal with the new issue. Well, that's more time than you would have had if the issue had come up as an objection.*

32

Help the aged

The directors at the top of the organisation are usually older than most of their subordinates. This puts them at a disadvantage concerning new management techniques or technologies that have been introduced when they were already at the top. Their ignorance may be a problem for them, squire, but it's a cool career opportunity for you.

I once walked into the office of an old director on the day he had got a new computer. 'There's something wrong with it,' he said. 'I've been fiddling about with it for hours.

I have been through the start-up procedure in the manual and still there is nothing on the screen. I'll have to get the computer people in tomorrow.' I happened to know that there was a brightness button at the back of the new terminals, so I turned this up and the terminal sprang to life. 'It's pathetic,' I said, 'that should never have been left off when they delivered the terminal.'

I had done a lot for him in that moment. First, I had put the blame for his incompetence firmly with someone else, important for him not to lose face with me. Second, I had saved him from an embarrassing, though short, visit from the

Here's an idea for you...

It's absolutely true that if you look for unlikely opportunities in your working life they are likely to happen. Whenever you are talking to or listening to senior people try to find an angle where you can help. Listen for a statement like, 'we need to look into this' or words to that effect. Do a bit of research on the topic in question and send it to them with an offer to find out more.

Try another idea...

To see more about the psychology of this look at IDEA 27, *Vain, who* moi?

IT helpdesk, and third, I was in a position to show him round the new system further and we spent a happy half hour doing just that. But mainly I had put him a big step ahead of the other directors who probably also did not know about the brightness button, and who certainly were unfamiliar with the rest of the system. I could imagine the scene the next day as he, modestly, helped others to get started, and was congratulated by the chairman for getting to grips with all the replacement computer stuff so quickly.

Another incident raised an interesting dilemma for a determined careerist. An elderly director walked into an open-plan office I was visiting and made a beeline for a graduate trainee who had recently joined. He said that he been told that she might be able to help him create some slides for a PowerPoint presentation. 'Sorry mate,' replied our heroine, 'too busy.' The director looked a bit bemused and trolled off. I suppose the dilemma here is that if she had agreed it would have been apparent to everyone that she did not have enough to do. Well, maybe. I don't know about you but I'd just have helped him with his slides.

HELPING SOCIALLY

Here's an opportunity that dropped into my lap when I was in my late thirties. I had a meeting with the chairman of my company along with the MD and a few other folk. At lunch the chairman drew me aside, obviously interested in something I had said. He explained that his girlfriend, who lived in a flat in Mayfair (his wife lived in Wiltshire), was an ambitious advertising executive. She was pestering him for advice on preparing her 'objectives and key tasks', which she found hard to word. 'Been a while since I did that sort of thing,' said the Chairman, 'Could you help?' The upshot was that she and I spent a couple of hours thrashing out a great job description in the flat. He then joined us and said 'Well, you two have been beavering away, how about a spot of supper?' We had the 'spot of supper' in the Dorchester. Helping the aged definitely also helps the career.

For more on inventing a new job see IDEA 10, *Don't leave your job behind when you leave.*

Try another idea...

'With full-span lives having become the norm, people may need to learn how to be aged as they once had to learn to be adult.'
RONALD BLYTHE, writer

Defining idea...

How did it go?

Q **I went on a tour of our European offices with two directors, a man and a woman. I'm a first-line manager in a staff post and my job was to look after the admin, make sure they were in the right place at the right time and so on. I thought this an excellent opportunity. The female became very friendly and started to take my arm and introduce me to people as her 'treasure'. Now we are back she still gets me to do things for her and people are beginning to notice. She hasn't made a pass or anything but I still feel uncomfortable when she's around. Should I tell someone?**

A *It does depend on the circumstances; but I would probably go with the flow and hope that the relationship gives you a big career fillip at some point. The implications of what you do if she does make a pass are legion. Make sure you think them through beforehand and not the morning after!*

Q **I'm in exactly the position of the graduate trainee in your story. I've been asked to drive a director around while he is banned. It's not every day but it's quite often and if I keep on with it I'm going to get behind with my work. Should I ask him to find someone else?**

A *If all you are doing is driving him and then sitting around in the car park, I would be inclined to cut it to the minimum you can get away with. If, however, you are going to places with him and meeting lots of interesting people I would again be inclined to go with the flow. If it does cause problems back at the ranch you can always ask him for another job.*

33

Fail rich

A high-flying career by definition means taking some business risks. If you don't try you can't fail, but you can't succeed either. As you get higher up the organisation protect yourself against making a wrong decision yourself or suffering from a bad decision made by someone else..

One of the quickest ways to get rich is to fail at the top. It works like this: sign a three-year contract and then fail in the first six months. With luck you'll walk away with a million pounds for six months' work.

Klaus Esser, the last chairman of Mannesman, strongly advised his shareholders to reject the hostile bid from Vodafone Airtouch. In the end the shareholders decided to reject his advice. So does Herr Esser disappear into the sunset with a hangdog expression and three months' wages? Not a bit of it. According to *The Times* he received a 'golden goodbye' worth £19 million, of which 'more than half was agreed on the day the German company capitulated'. Mmm.

Here's an idea for you...

Some time back I chanced on the only way to make money out of a share in your own unlisted company. I once owned about 10 per cent of a company whose managing director assured us would be listed in three years, so making us very rich. I worked there for five years and he was still saying the same thing. By then I didn't believe him and decided to leave and go out on my own. To my amazement the two people who were in line to succeed me (you didn't think that one mortal could fill my chair, did you?) fell over themselves to buy my shares. They, of course, thought they were soon going to be worth a fortune, because the managing director had told them so. As far as I'm aware I was the only person to sell the shares for a reasonable sum of money. So, that's how to do it.

The Chairman of any public enterprise will inevitably fail eventually. Either he or she will preside over a major cock up (Marks & Spencer), or his or her shareholders will decide that someone else will make a better job of running the company (Mannesman). So what do they do? Easy, they use their own lawyers, at the company's expense, to draw up their contract with failure heavily in mind. They get the security of share options and bonuses round them. They certainly link bonuses to performance measures, but in the small print, and they also make sure that they get paid whether the performance measures are attained or not.

The total leaving package for Klaus Esser, again according to *The Times*, amounted to 43 times his final annual salary of £470,000. Nice one Klaus.

IF IT'S GOOD ENOUGH FOR THE TOP HONCHOS, IT'S GOOD ENOUGH FOR YOU

If someone tells you that there is no possible negotiation on your salary and package assume immediately that they are not telling the truth. After all, business is about negotiation. If someone tells you that you're grade 4 with two years' experience at that level, and that, therefore you are worth exactly the same as every other grade 4 with the same experience, either you are a data entry clerk, or you put the tops on baked beans tins in a factory, or they're lying.

If you want help in presenting the case IDEA 31, *Make them agree fast*, tells how to put pressure on without being tacky.

Try another idea...

So, negotiate in exactly the same way as they do at the top. Examine incentive schemes and make sure that you will get paid whether the targets are hit or not. Make sure the exit terms are generous if it all goes wrong. You are choosing to work for your organisation, so the least you can do is get the best return you can.

THE TRUTH ABOUT SHARE GRANTS AND OPTIONS

'The sin of hubris is inevitably and inexorably followed by Nemesis.'
ROBERT TOWNSEND, Avis CEO

Defining idea...

Let's face some hard facts about share options. We know that the value of a share is what the next person will pay for it. We know that what the last person paid for it is a reasonable estimate, if nothing changes, of what the next person will pay for it and therefore of its value. It's OK to go for share options when the shares are listed and there is an easy trade in them. Don't value them too highly in your salary negotiation; but you can value them.

But this is just not the case for a non-listed company. They have never changed hands except when the founders generously offer them to people they want to attract into the business. There is no next person to buy them, and there is no indication of value from the last person to buy them. You can therefore value them very accurately; they are worth nothing at all. Remember that in the negotiation.

'Let us never negotiate out of fear. But let us never fear to negotiate.'
JOHN F. KENNEDY

Defining idea...

If all the business plans I have seen had come to pass there would be millions of companies listed on the stock exchange. But usually the exit strategy does not work and the shares are never listed. Venture capitalists can make it happen because they back so many runners – and even they have *far* more failures than successes.

How did it go?

Q **I've been offered shares in a small business as a tempter to join them. Their exit strategy is to sell the company to a big company within five years. It's right to give some value to that as part of the proposition isn't it?**

A *In a pig's arse friend. Don't take any notice of the shares when deciding whether to join them or not. It's like making a life plan where some of the decisions you make allow for your winning the lottery.*

Q **How do I make the case for getting my bonus even if the target is not made?**

A *Look for things that are not under your control and make the contract pay the bonus if some other people don't perform or something else outside your control doesn't happen.*

34

I'm alright, it's the others

You can't build a career by blaming those around you for any failure to perform. Assuming leadership implies taking responsibility for what your team delivers. You lose credibility with your boss if you blame your team, and it's hugely demotivating. Break out of the blame culture.

This is a simple concept with quite a complicated twist. Let's keep it simple first. What do maintenance engineers do when they go out on a call to an upset customer? They have a survival instinct that compels them to look around for someone else to blame.

They blame the product – you know how it goes. 'Oh no it's an R567I, they're buggers to fix. Look at this, when they brought out the new model they saved money on the controls by altering the old ones rather than bringing out new ones. That's why it's so difficult to use. See, if they had put that there you would have been able to change the settings like that.' Or they blame the company. 'Under the

Here's an
idea for
you...

Most people wait to have their authority increased before they take on new responsibilities. This is slow-lane career thinking. Find something in your organisation that needs fixing and just do it. If you don't have the authority and your action plainly has a good result then you have probably expanded your responsibilities. (You may have to smooth a few ruffled feathers, but so what?)

old management I would have been here two days ago like you wanted. But since the merger, they've cut back you see. Frankly, the lists I get in the mornings need another bloke. But they won't listen.' And so on.

Now let's take this one stage further. It's quite easy for an account manager with an external customer, or a liaison manager running the bridge between two departments, to develop a close relationship with his opposite number. They're close because that's the way the organisations want it. The problem comes when something goes wrong. In this instance a good liaison officer will take responsibility, keep in close touch with his customer and put his own time and energy into solving the problem. There is a temptation, however, for the customer to try to keep the friendly relationship going by diverting her accusations towards another part of the organisation. 'Look, Ken, it's not your fault. We've always known that this was a bit of a grey area for the company. They never really solved the whole problem and that's why this has happened.' Sometimes she'll go even further and suggest that you keep a low profile while she deals directly with the department who will eventually fix the problem. This is dangerous talk, and the manager who falls for it is actually behaving in the same way as the maintenance engineer.

Now let's push the phenomenon up to higher levels of management. I once had a boss who was completely disloyal to his team. When things went wrong he failed to act as the essential link between the person with the

If you are looking for clues about using that direct contact with the director have a look at IDEA 32, Help the aged.

Try another idea...

problem and the member of his team responsible for coming up with an answer. He used me to give people bad news. I gave presentations of our plan when he was not sure what the high-level reaction would be. On one occasion he put me into a very difficult discussion that ended acrimoniously. He then worked out another way of doing things that met all the objections and, of course, presented that himself.

I thought he was getting away with it until his boss, the sales director, put his arm round me one day and told me that he had noticed that I seemed to be in the front line when the bullets were flying and my boss was only around when the battle was done. That was very useful. I now had a direct line to the director and he regarded my loyalty to my boss and my endurance in tough situations as good news for my career. My boss, he regarded as a maintenance engineer.

'A man who enjoys responsibility usually gets it. A man who merely likes exercising authority usually loses it.'
MALCOLM FORBES, publisher

Defining idea...

141

How did
it go?

Q **Well, I freely admit that we operate in a blame culture. It gets the job done. So what?**

A *In theory that will eventually cease to be the case and there will be a crisis, either of key people leaving, or of severe customer dissatisfaction. Look at the stress levels is in your organisation. There is now sound evidence that stress and continuous pressure eventually cause severe organisational problems. Someone will sort it out eventually. Instead of just sitting there, why don't you suggest to your boss that you do some research and analysis on the culture of blame?*

Q **I have made an implacable enemy by following your suggestion. Without the authority I purchased some office equipment the lack of which we had all been bemoaning for a long time. My boss thought it was a great idea, but there's a bloke in purchasing who has gone on record as wanting to stick a red-hot poker into something apart from the mulled wine. Have you changed your mind about never creating enemies?**

A *I hope I've never given that advice. I may well have said that you should not create an enemy unnecessarily; but it is next to impossible to have a high-flying career where everyone stays your friend. Nobody said life was easy.*

35

The multi-headed decision maker

In your career you'll have to sell yourself and your ideas to little committees. The challenge here is to see the situation from the various points of view of the members. Here's a way of getting many heads to nod at once.

People have different requirements in the same situation

When you go for a promotion you'll generally encounter at least three individuals. There's the senior manager whom I like to call the decision maker. Working for her is the manager to whom you will actually report, and then there's someone from Human Resources. Each of them reaches a conclusion from a different standpoint. The manager is making sure that they can trust and work with you as well as whether you are up to the job or not. The guy from HR confines himself to advising whether or not you have the skills and experience to do the job well. So what about the decision maker? She is, of course, contributing her experience to her manager; but she is also getting to know you better and deciding if you may be the sort of high flier that she needs.

Here's an idea for you...

What can you do in non-interview situations where you have to persuade a number of people to make a decision in your favour? Try the cup of coffee close. If it feels good and the vibrations are positive, offer to leave the group on its own for ten minutes. 'Look it must be difficult for you to make a decision while I'm here, I'll go and have a cup of coffee while you have a chat. I'll pop back in a few minutes.' Either they are going to agree to your suggestion, a buying signal, tell you it's not necessary for you to go, another buying signal, or they are going to say that it is not necessary for you to return and that they will get back to you in due course, probably a warning signal.

The cup of coffee close is quite fun if they agree to your returning in a few minutes. If everyone looks at you when you come back in they have gone for it. If only the chairman is looking at you and some people are having their own quiet discussion you can be sure you have more work to do or that you have lost.

PREPARING TO IMPRESS PEOPLE WITH DIFFERENT REQUIREMENTS

In your preparation for the interview you need to think of what each party is looking for. First of all take HR. To prepare for them you need to know the rules about grades, training and experience. They also tend to ask some pretty stock questions like 'What, Ken, would you say were your main strengths and weaknesses?' If you are not familiar with that sort of stuff, check out some of the vast number of books on interview questions and techniques.

It gets trickier when you think about your potential manager. He'll get advice on whether you are up to the job, and anyway his natural leaning is towards the question of trust. Are you being sincere? Can he rely on your loyalty? Are you just using this as a stepping-stone or will you actually do the job for long enough to make a difference? To help him out it's a good idea to ask questions. It's a much better idea to ask him about the job than it is to ask HR about the pay and conditions. I know that's obvious, but lots of people do it. They even ask if they can continue with their current holiday plans, for goodness sake. Do that sort of thing after the interview.

We look at a process for being persuasive in IDEA 31, *Make them agree fast.*

Try another idea...

Finally, and probably most difficult, is the decision maker. She has to think you are shaped like a bullet at the same time as the manager is getting the impression that you are going to settle down for two or three years at least. I think the best way to handle this is to make any ambitious noises at the start of the interview. Then talk for the rest of the time as though you know that you will have to stay in the job for a while to get the experience. As long as you have scored the point with the senior person up front, she will ignore what you said later if she chooses to move you on in six months.

'A committee is a group of people who individually can do nothing but as a group decide that nothing can be done.'
Attributed to the American humorist, FRED ALLEN

Defining idea...

How did it go?

Q **I went for an interview for a senior job in local government and ended up facing two politicians, one from each of the two main parties. These guys clearly hated each other? How should I have dealt with that?**

A *With enormous care. In my experience it may not be as bad as you think. Behind the scenes and away from public or press politicians frequently co-operate quite well with one another. But you're right to be cautious. I have sat there like a lemon trying to sell things to politicians who have totally lost it and are yelling completely irrelevant threats and allegations at each other. The key here is the chairman. Don't try to intervene yourself. If a row kicks off, the chairman should bring them to heel. If the chairman is slow to act, politely ask him or her the relevance of what is being said.*

Q **I was in this situation when the woman from personnel claimed that I needed more financial knowledge to do the job. The way she did it was a showstopper and the interview didn't last much longer. Look, I know more than enough about finance to do the job. How could I have stopped her causing them to make a mistake?**

A *Very tricky. Two possibilities – the first and my preference would be to take her on. Just refute what she is saying, and put up some evidence to support that point of view. Alternatively you can offer to do whatever is necessary to put the deficiency right; but I think this is weaker. Also, sorry, but I think something's gone wrong in your preparation here. You should have known about and pre-empted this issue.*

36

Two heads are better than one

Top people need to have two heads. You won't get to the top unless you pay attention to your operational goals, and you won't get to the top unless you think way, way ahead.

You have to think strategically. You need to balance the pressures of today against the longer-term thinking required to build your business and your career. Here's the deal...

1. Without a long-term strategy you run the risk that decisions you are making today will have a negative impact on your results in the future.

2. But we have to stay real; we're also always under pressure to carry out urgent day-to-day tasks. You have to meet today's objectives and overcome short-term problems. You have to respond to your customers, whoever they are. Everyone is involved in such work and in operational, or short-term, planning. In a fast-moving environment it is little wonder that planning for the future tends to take second place.

Here's an idea for you... **Identify a member of your team who is basically good at producing short-term results. Explain to her that you are going to develop that skill by delegating an increasing amount of today's targets to her. Do it and free up your time to develop a long-term strategy, particularly a long-term career strategy.**

3. The situation is very stark in start-ups and small companies. There is no point in defending an action as being right for the long term if it makes the business run out of cash. On the other hand, making a sale that is outside the main route you have planned could be catastrophic for the future. Brilliant careerists take this philosophy into large company planning too.

DEVELOPING THE SECOND HEAD

So we come back to the two heads. The leader of any team needs a 'can do; do it now' attitude. You need to be able to discuss a problem, find a solution and immediately pick up the telephone to start implementing the solution. No one has solved the particular problems you are facing now. You're breaking new ground here so one of your two heads has to look for solutions or activities that less dynamic managers might describe as completely off the wall.

Try another idea... **Now you have the time, IDEA 9,** *Know what to say to whom,* **gives some thoughts as to how to use it careerwise.**

And yet, and yet, no one built a business without an eye on the future shaping what we do now – the second head.

The reason for being pleased is in IDEA 2, *Don't bury them in advice.*

Try another idea...

Some people can keep the two heads going at once, reacting, ducking and weaving with the best of them, but also from time to time checking that they are not mortgaging the future or taking short-term measures that endanger the long-term goal. Others form teams of two where one person is clearly the go-getter, and the other the 'just a minute, let's think this through' person.

You may well have a leaning towards one of these methods. Don't forget, though, that eventually you need to be the forward thinker. Top people get others to sort out the fires and you're heading for the top. And that's the clue. You can get ahead very fast in the lower echelons by producing clever and rapid short-term results. But you have to grow.

In preparing for battle I have always found that plans are useless but planning is indispensable.
DWIGHT D. EISENHOWER

Defining idea...

How did
it go?

Q   **I've been doing this delegating the short-term stuff for a few months. What's now happened is that my deputy has made a huge mistake that threatens one of our major annual objectives. What's the use of this idea if I have to indulge in hands-on crisis management for the next couple of months?**

A   *I said delegate responsibility not abdicate it. You didn't hand over your job; you handed over the day-to-day running of it. You should have kept better in touch so that you would have seen the problem coming and put your deputy straight. Delegation allows people to make minor mistakes; if you let someone hit a rock before you intervene you're just abdicating responsibility.*

Q   **I like this idea because I've been moving in this direction for a while. I made it much more formal and documented the delegated authority. The person I delegated showed it to my boss who clearly was impressed that I had the confidence in her to do it. She is now angling either for my job or a promotion. Is that what you expected?**

A   *'Fraid so, yes. This is exactly what happens and you should be pleased. Look for your next move and make room. If the timing for that isn't right you'll have to develop someone else or persuade her that waiting six months for your job is a good path.*

37

A triple-whammy career boost

Taking an innovative idea to a customer and helping him implement it has three positive impacts in career terms. It gives you high-level exposure as loads of the customer's managers take responsibility for the initiative. It sells you and your products and services to your customer. It gives an opportunity for your lot to get on the bandwagon too.

Anticipating a customer's needs can pay all sorts of dividends.

A few years ago a major book retailer was planning a summer campaign to sell business books at airports and railway stations. The marketing strategy was to attract business people to take a business book on holiday with them. A publisher's saleswoman, who had an excellent relationship with her client, came up with an innovative idea. She suggested the retailer commissioned a new book, not too serious but nevertheless a business book, to attract people into the business section. The retailer loved it.

The publisher assembled all the main ingredients. It was to be a 7 x 7 inch book so that it fitted on the end shelves in the bookshops facing you as you enter the store.

Here's an idea for you... **Right, thinking caps on. Look closely at what your customer is trying to achieve. Look at what their competitors are doing. Study their trade press. Talk to other people in your organisation who provide similar products and services to their customers. Use the internet. From that research, come up with an innovative idea to take to the customer.**

The book was designed to look like an easy read with a large typeface and plenty of white space on the page. Because they'd fixed the size and font they knew how many words would be in the book, around 50,000, and therefore what it would cost and how much they could charge – a straight tenner. Not £9.99 but a clean deal at the checkout. It's yours for ten pounds, one note.

The retailer's middle management then had to sell the idea to top management. Most book retailing doesn't involve wads of money up front, but this project required real investment. The deal was that the retailer would have exclusive rights to sell the first print run of the book, and the next two in a series, but without the normal sale or return deal. If the book didn't sell, it stayed in their warehouse; it did not go back to the publisher – a real benefit for the supplier.

A manager drove the project through the return on investment process that the company used, and after some time and a few glitches the budget was agreed and the project given the go ahead. There were now seven weeks to go before the book had to be on the shelves.

The saleswoman had cleverly spotted two types of need here – the things the organisation needed to do in order to meet its objectives, and the things that managers need in order to advance their careers, or give them an easy life, or do whatever turns them on. In the case of this book the needs neatly coincided. The organisation needed a book that would attract people into the business section, looked readable as a holiday book but could still be

There's a related financial idea in IDEA 52, *It's done what to profits?*

Try another idea...

put on expenses. Middle managers were looking for a bit of creative thinking that would ensure that they would sell more business books that summer and that they could boast about to their bosses, all the way up the line.

THE TRIPLE-WHAMMY BENEFIT PICTURE

The publisher was laughing all the way to the bank, since it is not often that they get a guaranteed sure-fire winner, and the book retailer was busy rewarding and promoting the three or four people who claimed, modestly, to be responsible for the innovative idea, *career benefit one*. The publisher made a tidy profit, *career benefit two*, and there was a huge party with senior management from both organisations coming together to celebrate, *career benefit three*. (I got involved because they asked me to write the book in seven weeks. And that benefited my career too! Thank you Mark.)

'Fashion is something barbarous, for it produces innovation without reason and imitation without benefit.'
GEORGE SANTAYANA, philosopher

Defining idea...

153

Q **OK, I came up with something and the customer likes it. They are, as you predicted, clever clogs, selling it high and wide in their organisation. How do I let their top people know that it was my idea?**

A   *You don't, you fool. This is brilliant. Let them take all the credit. You have told your management that it's your idea and at this stage that's all you need. If later on you want the customer's management to know the idea's source you can get your boss to leak it to their top brass. But you only really need to do that if you are interested in a career move to the customer. Otherwise let well alone or you will lose the co-operation of their middle managers.*

Q **Same situation, later on. At a meeting with my boss, the customer told a blatant lie about how they had come up with the idea. What do I do in that case?**

A   *Smile, damn you, smile. I refer you to the previous answer. You are in an even stronger position now, since you and the customer both know that you know that they told a lie. Think of another idea – they'll have to do it now.*

38
Check what it's all about

There are two career reasons for reminding yourself what a manager is for. It is useful in operational performance because it checks that your focus is still lethal. In interviews it acts as a backdrop, as you illustrate what you have done to date, and what you will do in the new role.

What am I supposed to be doing? It's easy for second-line managers to get a bit disillusioned. They are close to the real action but not yet on the bridge.

One such manager I know, when asked to define his job, said 'In this organisation, I take material from my physical and electronic in-boxes and transfer it to my out-boxes. Sometimes I read it and add to it, and sometimes I don't bother. It doesn't seem to make any difference.' Is that really it? Probably not, so let's get back to basics of what you, the manager, are about:

1. You're there to enable your people to give of their best.

2. You're there to implement corporate and divisional strategy, but you can always see how what you're doing fits in with the bigger picture.

Have a look at your diary and your to-do list. Can you fit all your activities into these bullet points? If you can, you are probably carrying out your role as your boss would expect. If you can't, you may have lost control and be in fire-fighting mode. Think about how to get back on top of things. On the other hand, you may be a genius, in which case you make your own rules and operate outside the norm.

3. You've got a part to play in influencing high-level strategy. First-line managers are the voice of their people, markets and suppliers. They see day-to-day changes and are in the best position to challenge or alter the way the organisation functions.

4. You're a skilled resource to your team, and you add to their value. When a sales manager goes to see a customer, for example, the plan must make them do or say something that could not be done or said by the team member. A good example is when a production manager visits a supplier and introduces the topic of the environment and other green issues.

5. You know how the organisation works and so can add to the efficiency and productivity of your team.

USING 'WHAT A MANAGER IS FOR' AT AN INTERVIEW

Don't spend too much time banging on about your past record. You're being testing for your next job not marked for your last. At some stage you can use these points to show that you have thought about what a manager is for. Remember KISS: keep it simple, stupid. And get the level right, a mixture of pragmatic efficiency and energetic, wide thinking. To make sure you are talking widely enough, check that you have used an illustration of points 3 and 5.

IDEA 36, *Two heads are better than one*, can help the persistent fire-fighter.

Try another idea...

'A manager's job should be based on a task to be performed in order to meet the company's objectives...the manager should be directed and controlled by the objectives of performance rather than by his boss.'
PETER DRUCKER, management guru

Defining idea...

How did
it go?

**Q   It's all very well for you and Drucker to pontificate, but my boss
does control me. She is obsessed by the management accounts
and has a go at me when I vary from budget. The fact is the
system is up the creek and I have to spend hours and hours
correcting charges attributed to me wrongly, errors in the timing
of income and expenditure and so on. Can you think of a way out
of that?**

A   *No, I can think of three. Try just not doing the corrections. When she gets
on to you explain that they are just wrong and that you don't have time to
correct them any more. Go and talk to the finance people and see if you
can fix the problems at source. Offer to write a paper showing what the
management accounts should be like if they are going to assist your
performance instead of wasting your time. My inclination is to the first and
third of these. At least it means that something will happen.*

**Q   My team and I are bogged down in internal activities quite
outside the range of this idea. How can I persuade my boss to
scrap, for example, the activity reporting system that purports to
record everyone's activities on an hourly basis?**

A   *Explain to your boss that the undisciplined people with imagination just
make them up, and the conscientious people who fill them in correctly don't
need to have their activities monitored. Again, try junking them. You may
very well find nothing happens after the first explosion.*

39

Two, four, six, eight...

Who do we appreciate? A snappy career depends on a number of factors – performance, of course, but also reputation, what people say about you and whether they look forward to meeting you. Giving recognition to people's successes works at both levels.

Treat people as though they do actually exist and you might be surprised at just how well they respond to this.

In one of those television programmes where people swap jobs, the head of a PR and advertising agency changed places with the MD of a factory that made plastic bags. There was a very striking difference between the styles of the two men. The adman was touchy-feely and got on very well with his new staff. They loved him and started to make really good suggestions for improvements. The factory boss only had his job because he'd married the owner's daughter. The agency people completely rejected him and he looked like a fool.

I tell this story because what someone on the shopfloor said to their boss when he returned from the agency flabbergasted me. She told him that the thing she had noticed most about the other guy was that he had said hello to her in the mornings. The son-in-law had simply walked passed her as though she didn't exist.

Here's an idea for you...

This is going to sound a bit cheesy...but the next time you have a meeting ask at the start for everyone to talk for a moment about something they are proud of achieving since the last meeting. It starts the meeting off much more positively than the normal way, where the leading item is the biggest problem. Now suggest to your boss that they do the same. Honest, just try it.

In the 1920s a sociologist called Elton Mayo carried out an experiment with factory workers. He had a theory that people would work better in a brightly lit environment. He and his researchers installed more lights and turned them up. Productivity duly rose. To check his findings Mayo then turned the lights back down, and, guess what? Productivity rose again. In talking to the workers involved, Mayo came to understand that the reason for the improvement was this – the staff felt more valued and important because of the attention they were receiving from Mayo and his people.

Are you absolutely sure that you are giving people enough appreciation? Do you ever walk past someone in the company without even recognising that they exist? Do you always look waiters and other people in the eye and thank them for their service? OK, if you do, now think about your staff. Are they showing enough appreciation?

Finally we come to your boss. When was the last time you thanked him for the help he has given you, or for not asking you to do something he knew you didn't want to do?

IF YOU WANT TO BE RESPECTED, GIVE RESPECT

IDEA 11, *How do I look?*, has got more on the impression you make on people.

Try another idea...

It's easy when you say it like that. If you want to be listened to, do some listening. If you want to be appreciated, show your appreciation. Of course, you could be a person who objects to having to alter any of your appearance, behaviour or language in order to impress people who have influence over your career. Surely they should accept you just as you are and do away with this arbitrary, 'I thank you most sincerely' nonsense? You are absolutely right. And while you sit smugly, secure in your political correctness, you can watch colleagues who are prepared to compromise and give thanks where it's due advance their careers and fulfil their ambitions. Over to you.

'Always show enthusiasm; never be intense.'
SIR ROGER HURN, Chairman, Marconi

Defining idea...

How did
it go?

Q **I have worked hard on this with my team. We now, for example, do start each meeting by asking everyone to talk about something they're proud of. What can I do about the one person in my team who never smiles, goes about his work in a totally analytical way and doesn't show his appreciation of his people? He believes it to be insincere to thank someone just for carrying out their function.**

A *You are going to have to change his behaviour. Send him on a personal development course. The exercises that they put him will at least prove to him that his behaviour is wrong. The other people on the course will sort him out.*

Q **Every time I show people some appreciation and thank them for their efforts, they ask for more money. Is that what's meant to happen?**

A *Who said the spirit of entrepreneurship was dead? Good for them. Don't be fooled though; they still want the appreciation whether or not it's followed by other sorts of reward.*

40

Be a dedicated follower of fashion

There is a delicate balance for the careerist – how much of the latest management jargon and fads should you use and how much should you pooh-pooh them as so much business school tosh?

Everyone agrees that the stock market moves because of emotional rather than rational forces.

Most people agree that there is money to be made out of going against any popular fad in buying and selling shares – being a contrarian in other words. There may well be a parallel in running a business. Take two strategic fads, the one to diversify in the 80s, and going back to core business in the 90s.

If you had been a contrarian in the 80s you would have gone into the 90s with a fit, slimmed-down business focused on its targets. This would probably have made you recession proof in the débâcle of the early 90s, with enough debt but not too much, and so on. If, however, you had gone against the tide in the 90s, you would have enjoyed strong growth but missed out on the revolution that increased the spend on IT and gave huge productivity and customer service benefits.

Here's an idea for you...

Try this little experiment. When you are sitting with a team of managers talk gibberish for a while. Use good Harvard Business School words and lots of jargon, but don't let it make sense:

'Well, a new paradigm will help strategically but unfortunately not culturally. Fundamentally I think that is what empowerment means, particularly given the high values the company wants us to take to the market place. You boot up the new paradigm, round up the counter-enthusiasts and get every one sensible to recast their strategy. This'll change, you see, and bring huge improvements in the whole dynamics of the organisation.'

Unfortunately the best answer to this question is:

- Keep abreast of business fads.

- Study those you feel might benefit your operation.

- Follow the ones that make objective business sense and leave the rest to the dedicated followers of fashion.

BUSINESS SCHOOL BANTER

The business theory world is a world of fashion. Management principles come and management principles go, but the careerist is forever. Sometimes ideas last for a decade or so. You should know what the flavour of the month is. Don't be too clever, or your senior managers may just accuse you of using management speak, rather than proposing practical solutions. In this regard 'holistic' is dangerous and 'e-synchronous supply chain' only for those who can really explain it simply via references to examples from their organisation.

At the moment of writing 'globalisation' and 'brand globalisation' are dead safe. My antennae tell me that 'empowerment' is slipping and being replaced by 'manage not as a policeman but as a coach and mentor'. 'Synergy' is everywhere; 'continuous improvement' is safe but dull, while 'strategic innovation' is the coming thing. Strategic innovation is easy enough if you explain the shrinking timescales most industries have to effect change. In the steel industry strategic innovation may be every twenty years, in the software industry you may have to review strategy every six months.

Keep it very practical. The board is looking for people who are good at making things happen before it looks for great thinkers.

Remind yourself about listening in IDEA 42, *Don't talk so much.*

Try another idea...

'**We must distinguish between a man of polite learning and a mere scholar; the first is a gentleman and what a gentleman should be; the last is a mere bookcase, a bundle of letters, a head stuffed with the jargon of languages, a man that understands everybody but is understood by nobody.'**
DANIEL DEFOE

Defining idea...

165

How did it go?

Q   **I did it. I read out that paragraph and no one demurred in any way. What's going on?**

A   *Actually as I re-read the paragraph, perhaps it's true and maybe that's why they didn't demur! It's certainly as sensible as some stuff I have heard in the training room. It is interesting that you were not challenged. Probably because your audience only listened to the first few words, and partly because it just could possibly make sense and they weren't going to admit to not understanding it.*

Q   **What do you do with a boss who is heavily into this stuff? I go to meetings and he and some others drone on about empowerment and so on. They never come to a conclusion. It's boring and it wastes my time.**

A   *Two possibilities. I prefer the easy one. Don't go to the meetings. The trickier way is to ask for the objectives and agenda to be circulated in advance. When they kick off you can refer to the agenda and ask what objective this conversation is about. Nah, I still prefer just not pitching up.*

41

You only need 20 per cent of them, you know

Careerism involves looking for more ways to shine than simply meeting your operational goals. Senior managers want to see you helping to improve the whole environment in which you work. This means managing change projects. Here is a way of checking on the likely success of such a project before you agree to do it.

There are two main reasons why change projects fail. Sometimes there are just too many management initiatives for any of them to be completed.

Such an environment is known by sceptics as BOHICA management – 'bend over here it comes again'. Avoid another initiative if BOHICA rules in your organisation.

The other reason is that the people who need to change the way they work resist that change like mad. That's why managing change can be so depressing. But there is hope. Research in production and other environments supports a rule of thumb

Here's an idea for you...

When you break up into work groups or task forces, either in the planning or implementation phase of the project, seed the agents of change in among the laggards. This is vital because if you don't take charge of the groupings, the agents of change will work together and you will lose their contribution to converting the non-believers.

that I've found. If you have to manage a change process you need 'agents of change' to support you. Agents of change are people who fundamentally agree with the need for change and have the will to go through the process themselves.

Here's an example from a division-wide exercise. I helped to produce strategic plans for all the power stations of a European electricity supply company that was preparing for privatisation.

Senior management knew that there would be fierce resistance to the changes that had to be made, and they decided to include the whole management team of each power station in planning the new strategy.

This gave us rather large teams of up to twenty people, but seemed the right way to go. The resistance differed from station to station and a pattern emerged. In the more progressive stations where, say, 50 per cent of the team could be regarded as agents of change, we could already see the first signs of success. If at the planning session there were 20 per cent, it was harder work but it could be made to happen. Below that it looked and turned out to be hopeless. And, of course there was one where no agent of change appeared, not even the station manager, and we failed there. So the 20 per cent rule is a practical one.

WEIGH UP YOUR CHANCES OF PULLING THE STUNT OFF

If you want to see how a team sets up a strategy quickly try IDEA 38, *Draw your own map.*

Try another idea...

So, before you start to implement change make sure you can name the agents of change and that they represent at least 20 per cent of the team. Gather them together if you can, and explain their role in helping you. If you're not sure you have that percentage, get a long-term illness or move or anything, but don't take responsibility in those circumstances.

When you hear a depressed manager talking about the daunting task of getting a hundred people to change the way they work, ask him how many will be supportive to begin with. If there are a lot more than twenty, try to get a bit of the action (along with a bit of the kudos). If it is less than twenty, just leave them, politely, to get on with it. Don't get involved or you'll find that depression is contagious.

'Most of the change we think we see in life
Is due to truths being in and out of favour.'
ROBERT FROST

Defining idea...

How did it go?

Q **I've been asked to consider managing a project to redefine how we assess risk. I have checked that more than 20 per cent of the people involved believe it's important we do this. But as I look at the profile of the agents of change they are all the most junior people. Almost all of the senior people think it's a waste of time. Does this make a difference?**

A *Er, yes, good point. I wouldn't be comfortable to go for a project with such a central impact on the business strategy without, say, 20 per cent of the senior people agreeing to help. Use your boss to get some of them onside or look for a way out of it.*

Q **I've taken responsibility for altering the make up of the standing committees on salaries for my department. I had well over 20 per cent very enthusiastic but a number of them were in a team that has been moved to a different department. This has reduced the number of believers to well below your rule of thumb. What do I do now?**

A *Bloody hell, what bad luck! Any chance you could follow the team that left? If not, negotiate with your boss to put the project on hold until you deliver a few more converts.*

42

Nothing can go wrong, because nothing is planned

In days gone by, project management was the business of engineers who had techniques to control complex sets of activities. Nowadays, careerists need to treat a fluid list of activities as a project. Make sure you don't have one arm tied behind your back before you start.

The old image of organisations comprising separate functions operating on their own is giving way to cross-functional teams, and it's a good career move to manage at least one.

Taking on a high-profile project, particularly a change project, once again gives you exposure high and wide in the organisation.

A lot of projects are doomed to fail before they start because the manager doesn't recognise the need to define and manage activities as a project. Here's the holy trinity of rules for announcing and managing a project:

Here's an idea for you... **Find something difficult that needs to be done, some major change that the organisation needs to make. Perhaps your boss hasn't thought of it or has thought it too tough, but he or she would be happy to take the credit for it. Offer to manage it, and deliver.**

■ The timescale from start to finish is more than a month, often a lot longer.

■ There is more than one function involved.

■ You do not have direct authority over all the people resources needed.

If these three elements are in place go to your boss and propose that she becomes the sponsor of the project. Outline your vision for how things will look once the project is complete. Make sure the timing is right. Before you announce your project, test for 'management initiative overload'. This is a syndrome that haunts many organisations that have too many initiatives going on simultaneously, none of which ever gets completed. Don't start something that you can't finish. Never fight a battle you can't win. You're going to run it high profile so it's got to be successful. If your vision is bold and useful enough your boss may cancel someone else's pet project to divert resources to your new one. This is excellent careermanship. If it happens, make sure you are the first person to sympathise with the thwarted colleague, 'but what could I do, you know what she's like when she has the bit between her teeth?'

KICK-START IT BY THINKING THE PROJECT THROUGH TO THE END

The key to the beginning of the plan is assessing the chances of success. Look for strong driving forces that, for example, close a competitive gap, or gain competitive edge. They are strong if they translate easily into sales growth and so on. Restraining forces include people's natural resistance to change and their current workload. Remember, most projects aimed at improving the working environment actually create more work for people. Weigh up these forces. If the risk, to business and career, is sensible, go for it.

Cross-functional teams are by definition made of very different types of people. Try IDEA 7, Lead with style.

Try another idea...

Finally think about roughly how much resource you will need and how available it is likely to be. Negotiate for this now, before you volunteer to take on the task.

CHECK THE STAKEHOLDERS

Make a list of all the stakeholders, people who will in some way be affected by the project – this will be not only your key team members but also your customers and possibly your suppliers. You've got to get them all on board sooner or later, so make sure the list is complete. Think about how much authority your sponsor has, and wriggle out of any project where the sponsor is totally incompetent at getting his own way, or hated sufficiently for people to want anything he touchs to fail.

'*At one time people were expected to simply get on with their job and not worry about the "whole" picture. These days people have to understand the whole of the business to ensure that they can work in a cross matrix way and are able to move swiftly across the business to areas of greatest need.*'
JOHN A. HART, HR Director, Powergen

Defining idea...

How did
it go?

Q **I worked out a plan to change something very important in our organisation, went through the resource requirement and went to my boss for a decision. She was very enthusiastic about the promised results, but wouldn't give me all the resources I need. How do I get out of the situation where I've got a commitment that I know I can't achieve with the resources allowed?**

A *That's bad. If you'd told me earlier I would have suggested that you leak elements of the project bit by bit, checking that everyone thought the use of the resource was worthwhile. You could have built in a lot of contingency resource so that when your boss cut it down, as they always do, it didn't wreck the chances of the project working. As it is, I think you need to decide when the project will be looking at its most promising and destined for success; at that time use a presentation of where you are now to find another opportunity somewhere else in the company. Don't hang around until it actually goes over the cliff.*

Q **I'm trying to get the job of managing a project to relocate three small facilities into one new office block. My boss says that I should go on our internal project management course. This takes up quite a lot of time. Should I do it or leave the relocation to someone else?**

A *You've answered your own question I think. Someone's going to do it and potentially deliver very high-profile success. The person who does it will have to talk to everyone! To be honest I think relocation is much easier than people make out. The difficulty is not the mechanics of the move, but the politics of where everyone ends up – and that's great fun. I do think project management training is very useful nowadays. I'd find the time.*

43

It's a bargain!

Negotiate for everything! Your career will benefit in two ways. Negotiating to reduce your costs and increase your sales is good for performance, and this experience helps you practice for the most important negotiation of them all – your job and salary

You better believe it, everything is negotiable. Negotiating is a part of our lives; we do it all the time. In fact we do it so often we probably don't realise that we <u>are</u> doing it.

If you have children you've probably already done some negotiation today. Imagine telling a child that anything at all is non-negotiable. Fat chance. You can learn a lot from watching children negotiate. They have no inhibitions, they are prepared to use the sanctions they have available to them and they are completely devoted to the present with no thought for the future. These are all negotiating skills we lose as we grow up.

Never go into any negotiation to 'see what they are going to say'. Prepare positively. If you're selling, look for reasons why the other person should see that your proposition has value, rather than why you should be allowed to maintain your

Here's an idea for you... **Ring up an internal department who supplies you with a service and complain about their prices. You are, after all their customer. If they say that the price is company policy, go higher up their organisation. Eventually you will get to someone who can vary prices. It may be tricky to steer such a change through the management accounting systems, but where there's a will there's a way.**

price. In this context negative preparation is a disease with commission-based sales people. Try it out. Give a salesperson the authority to offer a 10 per cent discount, and every deal done from that day will have the discount deducted; that's their opening offer.

PREPARE ALL ASPECTS, NOT JUST MONEY

Think widely in negotiation. Look for objectives beyond, for example, price. What else could you get from the other party? Now put those objectives into priorities. You will have some objectives that you must achieve, some that you are going to work hard to achieve and some that would be nice to achieve. Now think of the other person's priorities in the same way. In fact think about all aspects of the person with whom you are about to negotiate. The more you understand them, the more likely you are to find a solution they will deem acceptable.

When you negotiate, you use your own flair as well as your company's rules. Managers like people who are entrepreneurial and who know that sometimes they need to walk over the company's normal business processes. Such entrepreneurs are regarded as good, but run the risk of upsetting others who play by the rules. Strike a balance here if you want to impress everyone.

With your career and wide-thinking preparation in mind, go to IDEA 12, *Please Sir, can I have some more?*

Try another idea...

Listening is a key skill at the discussion stage. Look at it this way. If you listen more than you talk in a negotiation it almost certainly means that you know more about the other party than they know about you. This logically leads you to a solution that suits them. You already know the solution that suits you. The opposite of listening in negotiating is interrupting. When you interrupt someone you are telling them to shut up. You are demeaning their arguments and suggesting that they can't say anything useful to take the matter forward. Imagine if you told someone in so many words that nothing they can say is important. That's the message that interrupting gives.

'Nothing is illegal if one hundred well-placed businesspeople decide to do it.'
ANDREW YOUNG, US diplomat

Defining idea...

How did it go?

Q **I tried going to our IT people and complaining about how much they charged for our stock control system. They stonewalled all my efforts and swore that I couldn't get a cheaper deal from anyone else. On a whim, I got one of my people to price out how much it would cost to buy the software and do it ourselves. Guess what, it's cheaper that way by miles. Is it a good career move to call their bluff, or would the ensuing brouhaha be more trouble than it's worth?**

A *Call their bluff, mate. Ram it down their throats. You're on to a winner here. Your boss can use this to negotiate other parts of their service as well. Prepare it carefully and try to think of additional benefits apart from the cost of doing it yourself. That way you avoid circular arguments about what is included in IT's price.*

Q **Is it generally better to table your financial offer early?**

A *Depends. When I was selling my way was to plan what I wanted, try to distract the other side by conceding generously on minor points and hope the big ones slip through. The key is to listen first. Let them dig a hole for themselves. In one case I had planned to ask for fees of £10,000 per month, but I didn't answer the straight question of 'How much?' Eventually the client, after a preamble about how hard and competitive times were, asked us if we would mind working for a fee of 'just £20,000 a month at first' until he could justify a budget increase to his boss. The return on investment for lunch was high, and all I had to do was listen.*

44

Get your own way with a consultant

External consultants present both an opportunity and a threat to your career. Exploit the opportunity and avoid the threat by planning how and when to get involved with them.

You need to know your way around the consultancy jungle: these guys could make or break you.

The Economist said it all in February 1998. An article entitled 'Management Consultancy: the new witch doctors' declared 'If you had to pick a single business or profession that typifies the frenetic second half of the 20th century, it might well be management consultancy. It has grown fast…it is easy to get into…it pays well…and, best of all, nobody can agree precisely what it is.'

Ah, how the mighty are fallen. Since the turn of the century the consultancy world has dealt with many problems – a dramatic fall in demand, scandals such as Enron and customers who feel that they were ripped off and deceived by consultants in the past. Daily rates, or *per diem* rates as the snotty big boys call them, have

Here's an idea for you... **Is there a tricky issue where you're finding it hard to get your own way? Could an outside consultant help? If so, make sure the case for bringing in a consultant is well made.**

plummeted. At the same time many new consultants have set up shop. Many of these new freelancers were made redundant, especially from the large consultancies. They believe themselves to have many skills covering all aspects of business life. Few of them have many clients. Rude people call such executives who have gone out on their own as consultants the self-unemployed.

So the stage is set for the career person to cash in. Consultants cost less than they used to; so you can get flashier ones for the same price. They are hungry for work and they will tend to remember the people who hire them.

Arm yourself with the essential information:

- What is the purpose of hiring a consultant?

- What can an outside agency do that internal staff cannot?

- Can you justify the cost?

Now brief the consultant extremely carefully so that the answer they come up with is exactly what you first thought of.

USING A CONSULTANT FOR CAREER BENEFITS

As you know, one of the major issues that you have to deal with is company politics, the messy stuff that gets in the way of getting a job done. It is inevitable once you add the unpredictable element of people into any situation. You can use an outside consultancy firm to provide an unbiased view to the powers that be. The opinion may be more readily accepted than if it was something you'd come up with. And then there is always the added bonus that external advisers can take the blame for unpopular but necessary solutions to problems. Your reputation can stay intact.

Using consultants could be a really smart career move. Spend your company's money lavishly on them – everybody needs a pal and in any case consultants have to be kept in the style to which they've become accustomed. Such friendships then give rise to new opportunities in different organisations, because this is a two-way relationship. If a consultant has a client looking for a top person, and you've previously hired him into your current organisation at huge expense, they may very well introduce and recommend you. They need a pal too.

In thinking about consultants it is worth reminding ourselves of **IDEA 28,** *Everybody lives by selling something.*

Try another idea...

'**Here's the rule for bargains: "Do other men for they would do you." That's the true business concept.**'
CHARLES DICKENS, *Martin Chuzzlewit*

Defining idea...

181

How did it go?

Q **Right, I got a bloke in to look at an organisational problem I wanted to resolve. It meant some blood on the walls so I wanted cover and strength from an outsider. I hinted broadly at him that he should not go near my boss. So he went straight to my boss's boss on his first day. Why didn't you warn me this could happen?**

A *Sorry about that. It didn't strike me that anyone would believe any assurance from a consultant that they would not seek a higher level of contact. Career people like you would do it if you were in his position, so you should expect him to. It is much better to control their access than try to block them. Take them in to meet senior people when there is a purpose and, of course, assume that you are going in with them.*

Q **I was talking to a consultant hired by one of my clients. I believe they needed to talk to me in order to carry out their brief. They were very iffy with me and basically saw me to the door. How should I have got to make my point to them?**

A *Get yourself introduced by your client. If you blunder about with a consultant with as high or higher a level of contact, then you'll get into trouble. Get your client to write in the consultancy specification that they need to talk to you. Either that or get them to write a note to the consultant indicating why they should meet you.*

45

It's how you tell 'em

Getting people to agree to your plan of action often requires you to make a presentation. Here's a good tip for making the most important part of the presentation, the opening, effective.

Presentation — the big career boost. At certain points in your career you'll have to make presentations to senior people. If you have a natural talent for doing this, you put yourself way ahead of the competition.

In some customer cultures, indeed, you're pretty much up against it if your presentation skills are poor or if that rabbit in the headlight look lasts right through your presentation. Practice hard, always volunteer to be the person who presents the results of a workshop, or who makes the presentation on some new strategy to the departmental meeting.

I had no idea of how useful presentations were until the following incident. In the dark ages of the 1970s the business world in the UK was burdened with a new tax,

Here's an idea for you...

It is a very good, though simple, idea to announce exactly what you want the group to decide at the start of a presentation. The audience then knows where you are going to take them. Some people avoid this as you do run the risk that someone in the audience will tell you that you won't be able to get there but logically it is better to know this at the start of the presentation than at the end. Who knows, if you know what the audience's objections are, you may be able to use the presentation itself to overcome them.

Value Added Tax. I was a graduate trainee at the time and my boss, who sometimes found it difficult to think of constructive things for a rookie to do, asked if I could have a look at this VAT business and make a presentation to the next area meeting. I got hold of government papers but found the whole concept of the tax hard to understand. I persevered, spoke to a load of people, including government people, who were very helpful. At last I was able to understand how the tax worked in my terms. These were, of course, the terms that my colleagues in the area would also use. A bit of luck had me hear a joke on the radio about VAT inspectors being called 'Vatman and Robin', so I nicked that and used it as a running gag through my presentation. It went well and I knew that it had done me no harm at all. My boss mentioned its success to his boss, who had just sat through an incomprehensible presentation on VAT by a bunch of accountants. I was asked to give the same presentation to the management team at my boss's boss's team meeting – very useful, high-profile stuff, and a lesson in influencing people.

PRESENTATION TIPS

If you're not a natural at this game, get some training until you can at least survive, although I do know one senior manager who made it to the top and remained a complete liability on his feet. When asked how he did it he replied, 'ducking and weaving, old boy. I avoided presentations like the plague'.

Funnily enough the best tips for making effective presentations are the usual suspects. Set tight objectives and talk exclusively in the terms of the audience. It can be difficult to make the same presentation to the marketing people and research and development at the same time even when what you have to say is interesting to both. So try to avoid having to talk to audiences whose members come from different professional backgrounds.

It might be a good moment for all of us to brush up on complaint handling. See IDEA 22, *You've done what?*

Try another idea...

'*Presentations are about them, the audience, rather than you, the speaker.*'
Senior sales manager

Defining idea...

How did
it go?

**Q   You bastard. I was impressed with this idea and opened a
      presentation to the board on a good idea that I had had, by telling
      them what I wanted them to do. The chairman went mad. 'We
      rejected that idea ages ago. Under no circumstances do I want
      more time and work spent on studying it. We have thought about
      it and decided against it.' Then everyone joined in and I have done
      myself no good at all. Bastard.**

A   *I'm sorry you feel so upset about this and that a misunderstanding has left
     you in a perilous position. The idea of signalling the objective of the
     presentation at the start doesn't just replace normal presentation preparation;
     and that includes avoiding surprising top people. You needed to do some
     preliminary work with one or two of the people who are going to the
     presentation so that you can check out the positions that the top brass are
     taking. It's called lobbying.*

Q   This idea's as much use as a monk's dick.

A   *Please try it again but prepare the ground carefully.*

Q   Bastard.

A   *I think we should move on.*

186

46

Of course it's risky

You must assess the risk of any project you have volunteered for. Remember, you're assessing the risk of the project to the business, but also, more importantly, to your career.

The opposite of delivering on time and within budget is to disappoint. Yet all successful career people emphasise the need to take risks. In business high return reflects high risk and that goes for your career too. But never promise more than you can deliver.

The business benefits of a successful project can be divided into three types. They are reductions in cost; avoidance of costs; and benefits, often improvements in sales, that occur because you have improved control. Let's suppose that you are preparing a cost/benefit/risk analysis for the finance people. Dividing the benefits into these three categories kills two birds with one stone. It will help you to understand the possibility of disappointment, and it will strengthen your hand with finance.

If you've gone through this simple analysis system, think about presenting the results to management. But remember that the name of the career game is risk management. Don't present the case you believe, instead present the case that shows the risks to be a bit higher than you actually think. Underpromise and overdeliver is the mantre of the ambitious.

Finance people probably think that reducing costs is paramount. (Avoiding costs is desirable too, but harder to achieve.) Companies are continuously re-engineering their business processes. Although this almost always ends up costing money, it is often justified by the fact that it affords management better control over the business. This may be good enough for the people running the business, but it is not sufficiently concrete for the finance department. They want to know how this benefit will turn into cash. No estimate for the future will be exact; risks to the benefits are that you will deliver less than your prediction, or that you will not deliver them in time.

Here is an example of a risk matrix using the benefit type as the grouping. As well as the most likely estimate, calculate the worst scenario and an optimistic one.

	Pessimistic	Most likely	Optimistic
Reduce costs	Likelihood 1	Likelihood 3	Likelihood 6
Avoid costs	Likelihood 2	Likelihood 5	Likelihood 8
Increase revenues or control	Likelihood 4	Likelihood 7	Likelihood 9

Experience allows us to give each cell in the matrix a number from 1 to 9 in the order of confidence that we should have that the benefit will be achieved. It goes from the most likely to occur, the pessimistic estimate for a cost reduction, to the least likely, an optimistic estimate for a benefit in increased sales or improvement in control.

ASSESSING THE RISKS OF DELIVERING GOOD RESULTS

In **IDEA 52**, *It's done what to the profits?*, you'll see how a very small change in costs and benefits has a much higher than expected impact on the bottom line.

Try another idea...

Assuming we know the costs involved in the project we can now calculate whether this is a high- or low-risk project. Add up all the benefits from the cells marked 1 – 3. If that produces a number greater than the costs, the project can be termed low risk. If you have to go down to 8 or 9 before the costs are covered you have a high-risk project. Think about wriggling out of it if you need to go as far as the cell numbered 6 to break even. At that point the risks are getting high.

In comparison with benefits, costs are more straightforward to estimate. Risks to the costs are that they will be greater than budget, either because your estimate is wrong, or because delay has cost money. You can add contingency money to the costs at this stage and see where in the risk matrix the necessary return is achieved.

Cost/benefit analysis is a closed book to the unambitious. It is therefore an opportunity for the careerist to show that you are willing and able to test your ideas against a logical benchmark. Add to it the career-protecting risk assessment and you have two management techniques to make your sojourn as a project manager, or a line manager with an idea, brilliantly successful.

Citizens, citizens, the first thing to aquire is money. Cash before conscience.'
HORACE

Defining idea...

How did it go?

Q **Following one of your big ideas, I felt myself very lucky when the managing director asked me to manage a project affecting almost everyone in the company. You referred me to this idea, and I did the risk analysis. According to your rules I need all the benefits up to square 9, in other words there is a high risk that this project is financially not worth doing. Should I tell her?**

A *Um, no. This is tricky. On the one hand you don't want to lose the opportunity of close involvement with the MD's pet project. On the other hand if someone, for example an accountant, looks at the numbers it could spell trouble. I think you could try the old 'a small percentage of a large number is a large number' ploy. Ask her the question, 'what is the major reason you want to implement this project?' Whatever she says, ask her where the benefit will come financially. Look for her to say something like 'payroll' or 'stock', anywhere where there is a big number. Then suggest that the benefit can't be less than 2 per cent of that big number and put that into the equation. No one will be able to gainsay it before or after.*

Q **Right, I have finished a small project and I can just about sort the benefits into your categories. Is it a good idea to publish the results?**

A *This is not a difficult question. If the results are poor, keep quiet; if they are good, tell the world and his dog.*

47

Be successful whatever your gender

It's easier to get to the top if you are a man than a woman. Here are some women's thoughts about how to deal with discrimination.

The statistics are depressing if you are a woman. Look at the number of female MPs; look at the tiny number of women who make it to the boardroom and the number of female CEOs of blue-chip companies. You would never believe that there are more or less the same number of men and women in the world.

If you want to change this in general by politicking to remove barriers and discrimination against women, do it in your spare time. If you are a career woman, look at it as a personal challenge, not a male plot, even if it is. Your job is to get to the top not to make the world a better place.

Here's an idea for you...

Career women also agree on another hugely logical suggestion. They say that childcare problems are probably more stressful and difficult to manage than the jobs themselves. Why don't more employers set up first-class facilities for the children of employees? If a mother knows that her babies are being well looked after, that medical care is available at the workplace and that she will not be dragged off if, for any reason, a child is sent home from school that day, she is likely to perform her job better. Look at your organisation in this regard and see if it is not a good career step to put up a paper with this in mind. (Particularly if one of the senior recipients of this paper is a woman.)

Defining idea...

'Women who seek to be equal with men lack ambition.'
THOMAS LEARY, psychologist

I am not a woman; so to write this idea I have spoken to a number of successful women and condensed their wisdom.

BE ECONOMICAL WITH THE TRUTH

A TV programme not long ago carried this message: if you are a woman in your late twenties or thirties, you are likely to be discriminated against if you go for a promotion or for a new job. Managers are prejudiced against these women: if they have children they may have to take some time off to look after them; if they do not have children then they may take maternity leave in order to start a family. The discriminators are not only men, but also women who are themselves opting not to have children in their thirties.

This is surely an occasion for women to ignore the strictures of Robert Townsend never to con anyone, or this book's advice not to lie on your CV. Lie your head off. Leave the kids out of the equation. Perhaps you might hint at the fact that it just isn't to be, and that in the circumstances you are going to channel your energies into a career rather than a family. This is probably not very good, but you will be able to improve on it. Economy with the truth was the preferred tactic of many of the women I spoke to.

IDEA 3, *Be seen to make good suggestions*, might be helpful at this point.

Try another idea...

Women have given me other suggestions for what to do apart from lying your head off:

Put off becoming a parent until your 40s (you can always freeze your eggs).

Have children and get your partner to stay at home while you cultivate your career.

Smack down the people who defend the current situation. They tend to say that maternity leave and taking time off for the kids discriminates against shareholders by damaging the profits of the organisation. This can't be true, can it? For a start it seems more damaging to the shareholders to ignore the talents of half the managers in that age group. (Frankly, I know some male managers whose general incompetence would probably kill a baby left in their charge, so goodness knows what they are doing to their businesses.) And who are these shareholders? In the end most shareholders are people building pension funds or they are pensioners themselves. If there are more men building pension funds than women, then this is a result of this discrimination, and there are certainly more women pensioners than men. Pensioners live off the equities built up in their pension funds; therefore giving equal rights to women managers cannot damage the interests of shareholders. QED.

> '*It is not the glass ceiling that holds women back from rising high, it is the children hanging on to their hems.*'
> POLLY TOYNBEE, journalist

Defining idea...

How did it go?

Q How can I lie about the fact that I've got kids? It's bound to come out when I have started in the new job and then what?

A *Good point. What women said to me was that by the time they find out about the kids you will have proved yourself and they will need you to continue in the role. They also said that it is much easier to get away with discriminating against women by not offering them jobs or promotions, than it is to avoid charges of discrimination if they get rid of someone.*

Q I'm a woman. I have an opportunity to move into a new part of my organisation that is very male-dominated. Do women find that sort of situation impossible?

A *They told me that they had to work very hard to overcome prejudices at first, but that they won out big time in the end. If you join an outfit where women at the top are rare, an increasing number of men are scared that you will shout 'discrimination' and will positively do what they can to avoid it. And if there aren't any women around, who's going to be that one female representative on the board? Get in there quick, it could be you.*

48

Make me an offer

Once you get into a senior position much of your time will be spent in negotiation. Thinking about how you negotiate is key for your performance and for the terms and conditions of your post. Here are some insider tips on the delicate art of negotiation.

So you've marshalled your arguments, and both sides have laid at least some of their cards on the table. The fact that you are both still there means that you have tacitly agreed that your opening position is negotiable.

You have listened for signals that show where there's room for manoeuvre or compromise. At some point comes the time to make a proposal. Do it sensitively and tentatively. Don't look as if you are rushing. Imagine if someone selling you something came up with a proposal to discount the price before you had even asked. You'd smell a rat.

Here's an idea for you...

Try thinking up some minor points where giving in will make little or no difference to you. Then you can give them away. But remember to give concessions really reluctantly even in this case.

You may at this stage see an acceptable solution as a parcel of related items. Present it as such. Give your conditions first and then the parcel including their and your concessions. Never give anything away for nothing. If you are making a concession there must always be a condition. If you concede willingly, then you can be sure that the other side will notice and take it out on you.

Similarly in job terms, it's a mistake to go straight to the salary; much better to talk through job satisfaction, timing of review for promotion, pension, cars, office facilities, club membership, family health and so on. This puts the salary into context and gives both parties side issues to give and take on. You can at this stage be firm on those parts of the negotiation where you know that there will be no difficulty in their accepting.

GO HIGH

Your proposal will in the end become unambiguous and specific but you are looking for signals from the other side that they will find the eventual proposal acceptable. Strike a balance between a concrete offer and a flexible suggestion. A concrete offer once rejected makes the negotiation difficult and can at worst lead to deadlock. On the other hand, show too much flexibility and the other side will assume that you are prepared to give in every area. Your first proposal should be realistic, but on the high side. I have run a negotiating exercise in training events and found that there is a huge correlation between opening high and ending up with a higher than average result. Then move in small steps. (Why do salespeople think that the first number in a discount is 10 per cent? It's not; it's 1 per cent or 0.5 per cent if that makes sense.) It's often useful to link parts of a proposal together. 'If you will pay for the health club, I'll accept a lower scale of health insurance.' Give any proposal made to you some consideration even although you may want to reject it completely. Oh, and listen to the whole of the proposition – don't interrupt.

I am assuming that you are timing the whole negotiation properly. Check out IDEA 48, *Please, Sir, can I have some more?*

Try another idea...

Don't forget to write down all the points that you have agreed. It is an old trick to add one or two points in the letter of agreement sent out after the meeting, so make sure you have a comprehensive note of what was agreed.

One of my customers used to send me a draft contract. I would look at it and query some points. His custom was quite quickly to concede a lot of those points except where he was absolutely determined not to move. At that point he sent me another contract that I signed. It was only when we had a small problem later that I discovered his habit of changing other items in the contract as well as the ones that I had queried. I don't like such a technique since it runs the risk of making someone feel badly misled, but watch out for it.

'Only the paranoid survive.'
ANDREW GROVE, co-founder of Intel

Defining idea...

How did
it go?

Q   **I was in a negotiation and trying to do what you suggest, keep my first offer to myself until as late as possible. What do you do if the other side keeps asking for your offer, and appears to be getting waxy?**

A   *You will probably have to make your offer. Try asking them questions that help to reveal their own estimate; but in the end you have to answer their questions. Some people make it a rule to answer the second time someone asks the direct question.*

Q   **My negotiation was going very well. We had agreed salary and all of the minor points, and I was about to summarise when my boss suddenly introduced another element. She said that all was well provided I agreed to take on a person who nobody in the organisation wants because he's impossible to manage. I was tired and due to meet my boyfriend half an hour before this bombshell, so I gave in. What was the alternative?**

A   *You've half answered your own question. It doesn't matter how tired you are. When this happens (it's called a late hit by the way) you have to take it seriously and find the time to talk about it and get it removed. You should have told her that you had to take a ten-minute break to phone your boyfriend and put him off for the evening. Yes, the evening. This shows her that she can't give you the bum's rush on this. During the break consider the late hit as an opportunity? I mean if you successfully manage the unmanageable, think of the glory. Also, during the break, think out how she can help with the problem person. Once you have got a few concessions from her, take the person on willingly. Come on, you'll work out how to deal with the bastard.*

49

Make your team your wings and soar

The brilliant ideas you take to your boss and higher are only as good as the team which comes up with them, and your ability to exploit it in high places.

Some members of your team will come up with more helpful ideas than others. Make sure you are working with these people, rather than with your poorer performers.

It is much better to spend time with the bulk of your team, and try and get their average performance up. It is, after all, the satisfactory performers who will come up with the best suggestions. If you spend your time training and coaching them, preparing tools to help with productivity and showing them how to perform better, you may raise their average by a significant percentage. This improvement is spread across more people and your overall performance will take a big jump.

Now get them, rather than you, to present the new thoughts to your boss and higher up. Their enthusiasm will shine through and you will be seen as a great leader.

Here's an idea for you...

But what do you do with your low performers? This is a tough one, particularly if it is impossible or undesirable to fire them. The answer is also tough. Ignore them. Give them a strictly limited amount of your time. At best they will get the message and move on. At worst they will move on criticising you for being unhelpful. You will have covered yourself against this in advance by explaining what you are doing to your boss. And if he or she is spending too much time with their no-hopers they could be very grateful for your help.

Defining idea...

'**Always hire people better than you.**'
MARTHA LANE FOX, CEO
Lastminute.com

CAN YOUR CAREER COPE WITH EMPLOYING THE BEST?

There is another related issue here for the ambitious. Do you really want to surround yourself with high-fliers?

The upwardly mobile are always arguing about whether first-class brains in your team are an opportunity or a threat. I'm convinced that using the best people gets the best career results. They want your job? Then they'll actually have to perform, as well as try politically to look as though they, not you, are the inspiration behind the team's success.

200

Get good people under you both as staff and as consultants and pay them as lavishly as possible. A contented consultant has a boss who talks to your boss's boss's boss and has good credibility when he mentions how well you're doing. Well-paid staff are more likely to stay, and, of course, no one expects you to earn less than them. The other thing about the best brains is that they are in your industry and you never know when you might meet them again. Not in the short-term maybe but even ten years later people remember those who did them some good.

HR will have a set process for firing people. But there is a career implication too; check it out in IDEA 21, *Ready, aim, fire.*

Try another idea...

'If, in order to succeed in an enterprise, I were obliged to choose between fifty deer commanded by a lion and fifty lions commanded by a deer, I should consider myself more certain of success with the first group than the second.'
SAINT VINCENT DE PAUL

Defining idea...

How did it go?

Q **I have two problem performers. I have tried to cut down the amount of time I spend with them but their demands continue. They chase me down corridors and phone me at night. I can't fire them so what do I do?**

A *You are going to have to explain to them that you only have so much time for each member of the team. Arrange a regular meeting, say Tuesday morning, for a set amount of time and make sure the first few times this comes up that you have another appointment immediately afterwards. That should give them the hint.*

Q **This is all very well; but I have not one but two people in my team who look destined for the top. My boss knows that they come up with a lot of the ideas and suggestions that we eventually put in place. Surely there's a danger that I will not be seen as a key player?**

A *That's the point, you berk: you're not a key player, you're a key manager. Keep it up. Trust me, good leaders always make their people look extremely good as well. Quite soon they'll promote you to another team with problems to work your magic with.*

50

Well read

You need talent, artistry, political awareness and opportunism to enjoy the best your career can offer. You also need knowledge. This knowledge is much wider than your own industry. Here's how to get what you need to know.

Read external sources widely on and around your subject.

In trying to find out what makes great businesspeople tick, I asked a director of a large company what made his MD so successful. I had met the guy and knew him to be very clever and very quick. But what else was there to him? 'I'm not sure,' said the director, 'but I do know that he's in his office every evening until about 9.30.' 'What on earth is he doing?' I asked, 'Well, reading mainly. He keeps up to date with everything there is to read about the business climate, his industry and his customer's industry.'

Broaden your knowledge base. If you don't usually read a newspaper, get into the habit now. Try *The Economist* or *New Scientist* for a change. Perhaps a tabloid could give you some pointers on popular culture and what people are buying in droves.

Here's an idea for you...

Get a copy of your annual report and the annual report of your main competitor. Do some financial analysis of the two companies and see who is in the better state and why. If you cannot do this, go and see a friendly financial controller and ask them to help you, and give you some advice about how to improve your financial awareness.

INTERNAL ECONOMIC AND FINANCIAL KNOWLEDGE

Have you ever tried to argue with a finance director? They don't play fair. They have at their disposal an army of jargon, calculated, correctly worded, to wrong-foot any up and coming manager. When you are promoted into a new job, you have to make sure that you understand the financial implications of what you are required and what criteria you'll be judged by. Or would you rather compete with one hand tied behind your back?

It's a vicious circle. If you ignore the financial side of your job you'll start to lose control of the physical task. If you get behind with the administration it's only going to get worse. You must query figures that appear to be wrong, particularly cross charges coming in from other parts of the business or you could find yourself carrying a huge load of costs dumped on you by someone who has learnt their way around the system and has seen you coming. Even if there is no one in your organisation with such evil intent, you must not rely on internal costing systems, they are very difficult to get right and are notoriously inaccurate. The main difficulty is to make the systems keep up with changes in the organisation.

The point in the end, of course, concerns decision-making. You can make a decision that seems correct for the organisation but is financially wrong and vice versa. If you combine your functional skills with knowledge of the financial consequences of your decisions you are on your way to a great career.

If you want to check you know enough about your organisation's strategy you could try IDEA 18, *Find out what you're supposed to be doing.*

Try another idea...

'Looking back on my own career I think the one thing that perhaps helped me was the breadth of my reading about the oil industry and overall economic matters, in addition, of course, to being up to speed in the depth of knowledge to do the job of the moment.
SIR PETER WALTERS, Chairman, SmithKline Beecham

Defining idea...

How did
it go?

Q **I went to see our financial controller and she referred me to an excellent book by your good self on finance (*Smart Things to Know about Business Finance*, by Ken Langdon and Alan Bonham, Capstone) and it brought me back up to speed. Trouble is, how do you maintain the knowledge when you don't have to use it very often?**

A *You have to use it often, I'm afraid. If you can't bear to read it every day, you should at least read the Financial Times every Saturday. It's a particularly good day to read it because it has a summary of events of the week and as well as a good personal finance section that you'll find useful. Read particularly the company results pages. This tells you how companies are faring both financially and strategically. And when you've finished the FT, pick up the Wall Street Journal.*

Q **My financial controller seems to love problems. I only hear from him after something has got out of kilter. He then uses some obscure ratio to illustrate the point. I have to take his word for it and make the adjustments he wants. Is there anything I can do about it?**

A *Bastard. Have a frank exchange with him. Ask for his help. Creep around him until your nose is browner than a kid on the beach in Spain. You must get him on your side so that he will explain what he means and you can start to see the problems earlier.*

51

Life's a balance

It's your choice whether to be a workaholic pursuing your career at the expense of all other activities or to place a higher priority on family and leisure. Whatever you choose, here is a way of calculating whether you have the balance as you want it, or whether you have to make some changes.

I am grateful to Penny Ferguson, an inspiring trainer, for this simple but effective idea for checking life/work balance. There are 168 hours in the week of which you spend 56 in bed. This leaves 112 for living in.

Draw a three by three matrix of nine square boxes and write an activity heading in each of them. The headings will include some of the following:

Friends, relationships, family, alone time, spirituality, personal growth, health, hobbies, leisure, creativity, work – operations or maintenance, work – strategic thinking and planning, and any other areas of life that you enjoy or endure. If you need more squares just add them. Don't forget to add areas where at the moment

Here's an idea for you...

If you found it difficult to decide which areas you want to change, try another of Penny Ferguson's effective techniques. Produce a vision for yourself by writing down a description of the best six months of your life that you could ever have. Include where you would live, what holidays you would take, who would be there and so on. Really dream and then go back to the activity matrix and plan to achieve that vision.

Now ask yourself what you need to do to get this plan off the ground. Who do you have to tell about the changes you are going to make and so on? This, then, is the start of your activity plan. You have made a decision about your work/life balance; so commit now to implementing the changes. It's a great idea to talk to a friend about your plan. Make it someone who is not too close. They are more objective and should help you when you are drifting away from the plan or putting things off.

you do nothing but which you wish to get involved in.

Now list the number of hours in a typical week you spend in each of these areas, convert it to a percentage of 112 and write the percentage into the appropriate box.

That's your starting point. You may wish to check what you have written with your partner and a work colleague to make sure you are not indulging in wishful thinking. If the percentages are just what you want, well done, ignore the rest of this idea.

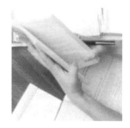

PLAN THE SITUATION FOR THE FUTURE

If you're not entirely happy with the result, look at the areas where you want to make adjustments. For every area where you raise the percentage you have to make a choice as to which area you are going to decrease. Add in any activities that currently you don't do and resolve to get started on them. Now translate the percentages into hours and see if you believe you have a feasible plan.

Read IDEA 8, *Actions speak louder than decisions*, to help to translate the vision into reality.

Try another idea...

'I did check my e-mails between holes but that depends on how important you think golf is. That's the nub of it really. If you regard golf as more important than work, you will put your entire effort into the game even when just hanging around waiting for the duffers ahead to get on with it. You get to be club captain but miss out on the chief executive's job.'
MARTIN SORRELL, Chairman, WPP

Defining idea...

209

How did it go?

Q **One of my resolutions is to spend more time with my daughter who lives half an hour away. How can I make that happen without seeming to coerce her?**

A *What's wrong with a bit of coercion? Make a lunch date, your place or hers, and tell her that you want to settle the next date at that lunch. Decide how many times a month you want this to happen and choose dates accordingly. It may seem a bit forced at first, but it is much too easy to lose touch with the blighters when they leave home. Formalisation of a regular meeting is the only way I've found that works. Is that OK? Put the book down and make the call now.*

Q **If I am to achieve my vision I need a lot more money. That makes it infeasible doesn't it?**

A *No. You need a plan to make some more money. Look for the first step. Do you need more skills or qualifications? Could you become self-employed? Think widely about it, discuss it with others then make your decision. If you think it's impossible you'll make it so; if you know you can do it, you will.*

It's done *what* to profits?

A thorough knowledge of the impact of dealing at the margins gives some excellent career-oriented opportunities. Make sure, first, that you and your team understand the havoc small items can wreak on a budget or profit and loss account and then use it to your advantage.

No doubt you'll often have heard people moaning about management removing some small perk that they have got used to.

There will be no more free biscuits at the free coffee machine; Fridays are no longer free fruit day; you can only travel first class on the train if you are with a customer; and so on. Such economies do seem rather petty, but they often have to be made. Why?

There are two ways of looking at this. First of all there is the budget point. Most managers' budgets consist mainly of the costs associated with employing people. This bill includes salaries, insurance payments, etc., and can be as much as 90 per cent of a manager's budget. It is rarely less than 80 per cent. That is why in looking for economies you have to deal at the margins with some pretty small beer.

Here's an idea for you... You can always improve your profit in the short term by stopping maintenance. If you're running a pub don't repair the chairs, stick the broken ones in the cellar. If you've got company cars put an embargo on servicing. This produces a one-off financial benefit that, because of the rule of 2 per cent can affect your profit and loss hugely. Be careful though. Make sure you're not there when the backlog of bills has to be faced – but with your new-found reputation for improving profitability it should be easy for you to soar onwards and upwards.

THE 2 PER CENT RULE

Here's the second way of looking at it if you are in a profit-making organisation. I heard it from a managing director. I can honestly say that I was completely gob-smacked with the simple logic, and that it has heavily influenced how I have run teams and businesses since. Take your profit and loss account, projected or historic, and adjust all the main subtotals by just 2 per cent. Here is an example:

	No. of units	Price per unit	Total
Sales	100	10	1,000
Variable costs	100	6	600
Fixed costs			300
Profit			100

The customer, you are informed by the salesperson, has a cheaper offer from a competitor. He thinks that if you could knock just 2 per cent off the price per unit, the purchaser can take a case for buying from you to his board. That discount plus reducing the order to only 98 units will make the customer's budget work.

The production department have had the agreement of management to a slight increase in the price of the unit; it's only 2 per cent, but in the circumstances you cannot pass this on to the customer.

Administration has been saying for some time that there would be a slight increase in their costs due to increased charges from the IT department. It's only 2 per cent.

You may find IDEA 44, *Get your own way with a consultant*, helpful in terms of persuading the team to co-operate for the six months.

Try another idea...

You know that these four changes to the proposition are all against the interests of your profit and loss account, but the numbers seem small, the customer has a lot of clout, and the salesperson is going to miss his target if he doesn't get this order. You agree to the changes.

Look at the actual damage this decision makes to the profit and loss account:

	No. of units	Price per unit	Total
Sales	98	9.8	960.4
Variable costs	98	6.12	599.76
Fixed costs			306
Profit			54.64

Each 2 per cent adjustment, all to your disadvantage, has combined to knock nearly 46 per cent off your profit.

Interestingly enough if you make the figures go the other way, you get a similarly dramatic impact:

*'O'erjoyed was he to find
That though on pleasure she
was bent,
She had a frugal mind.'*
WILLIAM COWPER

Defining idea...

Tell your boss you are going to sort out profitability over the next six months. Don't be too specific until enough time has passed to make you confident that you are going to succeed enough to demonstrate a difference. Towards the end prepare a presentation of what you did starting from the 2 per cent rule and going through the team contribution. With a bit of luck your boss will like it and get you to explain it at least to your colleagues, perhaps more widely in the organisation. You will not be terribly popular with your colleagues who dislike hair shirts but don't worry about it – you're on your way.

	No. of units	Price per unit	Total
Sales	102	10.2	1,040.4
Variable costs	102	5.88	599.76
Fixed costs			294
Profit			146.64

Right, how can you use this phenomenon career-wise?

Look at your projected profit and loss account for the next six months. Adjust all the subtotals by 2 per cent positively and look at the impact in absolute numbers. Resolve that the new number is your target for the period. Now get the team together in a conference room on-site. Explain what your new aim is and illustrate how the rule of 2 per cent works. Next tell them that there are times when it is right to spend the company's money lavishly but the next six months is not one of them.

Break your team into groups and get them to come up with ideas for expanding sales and reducing costs. Set these as the new targets and go for the big increase in profits.

Q   **My senior people didn't like the changes to their budgets that this idea requires. How do I get them to co-operate?**

How did it go?

A   *Ah, come on! Who's running this ship? Use the usual combination of incentives and instructions. For the ambitious, try hinting that they might get your job when this ploy is successful. For the rest, explain that it is only six months and that it's not optional. If you have to, use your boss, or even blame your boss for having to do it at all.*

Q   **It was going well until I told my boss towards the end of the six months. He hated the idea because it meant that other bits of his empire would look bad, and because he is a big spender and wants to remain so. How do I handle the fact that he has more or less told me to get my spending back into line?**

A   *What a bugger, the situation as well as the man. I'm afraid that it's risk-taking time. Go over his head. Leak the idea to his boss or even higher. You should be able to get it out without looking disloyal, but if the worst comes to the worst you should be in a strong position to defend yourself with your improved performance.*

The end...

Or is it a new beginning? We hope that the ideas in this book will have inspired you to try new things and encouraged you to take a long hard look at your career plans. You should be well on your way to seeing how to turn your OK career into a brilliant one.

So why not let *us* know about it? Tell us how you got on. What did it for you – what helped you punch through the plateaux and attain your career goals? Maybe you've got some tips of your own you want to share. If you liked this book you may find we have more brilliant ideas for other areas that could help change your life for the better.

You'll find Ken Langdon and the rest of the Infinite Ideas crew waiting for you online att www.infideas.com.

Or if you prefer to write, then send your letters to:
Cultivate a Cool Career
The Infinite Ideas Company Ltd
Belsyre Court, 57 Woodstock Road, Oxford OX2 6JH, United Kingdom

We want to know what you think, because we're all working on making our lives better too. Give us your feedback and you could win a copy of another *52 Brilliant Ideas* book of your choice. Or maybe get a crack at writing your own.

Good luck. Be brilliant.

Offer one

CASH IN YOUR IDEAS

We hope you enjoy this book. We hope it inspires, amuses, educates and entertains you. But we don't assume that you're a novice, or that this is the first book that you've bought on the subject. You've got ideas of your own. Maybe our author has missed an idea that you use successfully. If so, why not send it to info@infideas.com, and if we like it we'll post it on our bulletin board. Better still, if your idea makes it into print we'll send you £50 and you'll be fully credited so that everyone knows you've had another Brilliant Idea.

Offer two

HOW COULD YOU REFUSE?

Amazing discounts on bulk quantities of Infinite Ideas books are available to corporations, professional associations and other organizations.

For details call us on:
+44 (0)1865 292045
fax: +44 (0)1865 292001
or e-mail: info@infideas.com

Where it's at...